Contents

Encouraging Topic Interest

Help students to develop an understanding and appreciation of different media concepts by encouraging them to bring in examples of media to create a class display. You may also wish to conduct and display class surveys on media topics, or to compare students' media preferences.

Vocabulary List

Record new and theme-related vocabulary on chart paper for students to refer to during media literacy activities. During each new activity, encourage students to suggest words to add to the list.

Blackline Masters and Graphic Organizers

Use the blackline masters and graphic organizers in this book as appropriate for the level of your students. These reproducibles can be used to present information, reinforce important media concepts, and to extend opportunities for learning. The graphic organizers will also help students focus on important ideas, and make direct comparisons.

Learning Logs

Keeping a learning log is an effective way for students to organize their thoughts and ideas about the social studies concepts presented. Students' learning logs also provide insight on what follow-up activities are needed to review and clarify concepts learned.

Learning logs can include the following types of entries:

• Teacher prompts
• Students' personal reflections
• Questions that arise
• Connections discovered
• Labelled diagrams and pictures

Rubrics and Checklists

Use the rubrics and checklists in this book to assess students' learning.

Introduction to Media

Background Information

Media: Usually used to collectively refer to the most common forms of mass communication, including television, radio, newspapers, and the Internet.

Media form: The form used to communicate a message. Media forms include print forms such as a novel or brochure, and a wide variety of non-print forms as a blog, movie, podcast, television news broadcast, and product packaging.

Media text: Any text, image, sound, or visual representation (or any combination of two or more of these) used to communicate a message. Note that while many media texts do contain spoken or written words, some do not; for example, a photograph and a painting are each considered to be a media text.

Materials

Samples of media forms such as a brochure, flyer, menu, magazine, newspaper, CD, DVD, etc.

Blackline Masters

BLM 1: What Is Media? (pp. 6–9)

BLM 2: Introduction to Media——Prompts (p. 10)

BLM 3: Media Forms and Purposes (p. 11)

BLM 4: Media Word Search (p. 12)

BLM 5: Media-in-a-Day Tally (p. 13)

Graphic Organizers

GO 1: A Web Organizer About... (p. 110)

GO 2: Writing Planner (p. 111)

Assessing Background Knowledge

1. In a whole-group setting, display examples of media such as a newspaper, magazine, DVD, brochure, menu, and an open Internet website for students to view. Record students' responses on the board as the following questions are asked:

   - Can you name a few types of media displayed here?
   - In what ways are these types of media different?
   - In what ways are these types of media the same?

2. Ask students the following questions and record their responses on the board.

   - What is the purpose of media?
   - How do various media present their message? What are they trying to say?

3. Have students read and complete **BLM 1: What Is Media?** You might then have students return to the responses on the board to compare their ideas. This will provide an opportunity to correct any misconceptions. Explain to students that the items previously viewed and discussed are examples of media forms. As a whole group, talk about how each of the items communicate messages.

4. Introduce to students the term *media text* (see definition in Background Information). Reinforce with students that media messages are constructed using creative techniques designed to attract people's attention. Who created the message and why did they create it? Emphasize that different people experience the same media message differently. How might different people react to the same media message?

Identifying Types of Media

Invite students to identify examples of media texts both inside and outside the classroom. For example, students might suggest

- greeting card
- bulletin board display
- poster
- comic book
- website
- flyer
- magazine
- television show
- logo
- commercial
- newspaper
- sign
- billboard
- advertisement

Messages Without Words

Help students recognize that messages can be communicated without using words, such as through symbols and photographs. Give opportunities for students to look at a variety of symbols and associate a message. In addition, show students several photographs and ask them to explain what they perceive the message to be. Brainstorm a list of reasons of why people take photographs and why we have symbols around the community.

Understanding the Purposes of Media

Recall with students that every person who creates a media text has a reason for creating it. The reason for creating something is its purpose. Review with students what they learned about the purposes of media on **BLM 1: What Is Media?** Discuss with students each of the three purposes, using questions such as the following.

To inform

- What type of information would you find in a news article or newscast?
- How do you know if the information and source are reliable? What are some clues?
- How does the information in a magazine compare to the type of information you might find in a cookbook? Is it organized differently? Does it have the same number of authors?

To entertain

- What types of media are designed to entertain people?

To persuade

- What techniques are used in the media to try to persuade consumers to do or to buy something?
- How is the information presented? How are the people presented? Look closely at their body language and facial expressions. Do they look happy, sad, confused, or angry?
- In what ways do you think companies influence buyers to purchase name brands or clothing items with logos?

As a class, examine various media texts one at a time and ask students why they think the item was created. Be sure to ask students to use the clues in the media text to explain the reasoning for their choice.

Class Media Purpose Chart

Create a class chart, using the headings "Inform," "Entertain," and "Persuade" (or use other headings of your choice). As various media texts are introduced, have students decide where each one should be categorized. Students should soon realize that some media texts have more than one purpose. For example, a DVD about rainforest animals can inform as well as entertain.

Consolidating and Extending Learning

Use the following BLMs and ideas to consolidate and extend students' learning.

BLM 2: Introduction to Media—Prompts

Giving students an opportunity to reflect on the questions beforehand can lead to richer discussions, and encourage the participation of students who are often hesitant to participate.

BLM 3: Media Forms and Purposes

Use this BLM to help students consolidate their understanding of purposes associated with various media forms. Having students share their responses will help them recognize that most media forms can be used to achieve different purposes or different combinations of purposes.

BLM 4: Media Word Search

Reinforce familiar examples of media by having students complete this word search.

BLM 5: Media-in-a-Day Tally

By carefully recording examples of media they see, watch, or listen to, students can start to realize how much media makes an impact on their daily life.

Activity: Media Collage

Have students look through magazines, newspapers, etc., to find examples of media. They can then cut out the pictures and words, and paste them onto a piece of paper to create a collage.

Activity: Media Form Riddles

Challenge students to create riddles based on different media forms, such as

> I am a book that does not tell a story.
> You use me to find out what different words mean.
> What am I?
> Answer: A dictionary

Media Graphic Organizers

Use the additional graphic organizers found in this resource to compare a variety of media texts and their messages.

What Is Media?

What do people mean when they talk about "media"? They are talking about ways to communicate a message to a large number of people. These ways include television, newspapers, radio, and the Internet.

The word *media* comes from the word *medium*. When we talk about communicating messages, *medium* means "a way to communicate a message." Television, newspapers, radio, and the Internet are each an example of a medium—each is a way to communicate a message. But a medium does not have to communicate a message to a large group of people. When you make a phone call, the phone is the medium you use to communicate with one person.

Media Forms

We use different forms to communicate messages. We can communicate a message through words on paper, but there are many different forms we can use—for example, a letter, poem, brochure, novel, or an advertising flyer.

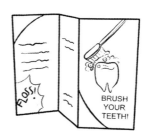

The medium of television uses many different forms, such as a news broadcast, movie, comedy or drama series, and commercial. The Internet uses different forms too, such as a blog or podcast. Many media forms you see on television are also available on the Internet.

continued next page ☞

Purposes of Media

People communicate messages for different purposes.

Here are three main purposes of media messages:

Purpose	Examples of Media
To inform (to provide people with information)	• newscast • news article • public service announcement
To entertain (to give people enjoyment)	• comic book • movie • cartoon
To persuade (to convince someone to do or believe something)	• television commercial • advertising flyer • letter to the editor

A message often has more than one purpose. A television commercial can entertain us by making us laugh, but it also has the purpose of persuading us to buy a product.

Brain Stretch

On a separate piece of paper, create a collage of images and words that show examples of different media.

What Is Media?

1. When it comes to media and media messages, sometimes you need to think outside the box. For instance, is it possible to communicate a message without using words? Look at the examples below and explain how signs and symbols can also send us a message.

a) _____

b) _____

c) _____

d) _____

e) _____

f) _____

2. Using your own ideas and information you learned from the reading, describe how media is used in daily life.

_____

_____

_____

_____

continued next page ☞

3. For Health class, Jeff wrote a song called "Please Eat Your Vegetables!" The lyrics are funny, but they also give people good reasons to eat lots of different vegetables. Jeff wanted to share his song with people all over the country, so he made a music video and put it on the Internet.

a) What are the purposes of Jeff's song?

❏ **Inform**   ❏ **Entertain**   ❏ **Persuade**

Justify your thinking.

_____

_____

_____

_____

b) What medium did Jeff use to share his song? _____

c) What media form did Jeff use to communicate his message? Do you think it was a good choice? Explain your thinking.

_____

_____

_____

_____

4. What is one television media form that you enjoy? Tell why you like it.

_____

_____

_____

_____

Introduction to Media—Prompts

1. What does the word *media* mean to you?

_____

_____

_____

_____

2. Why do you watch television, listen to the radio, read newspapers, and surf
   the Internet?

_____

_____

_____

_____

_____

3. Product packaging is an important way of communicating information about
   a product. What are some examples of the different types of information we
   get from product packaging? (For example, think about the information you
   find on the box for a toy, on a label for a tin of soup, and on the front and
   back covers of a music CD.)

_____

_____

_____

_____

_____

_____

_____

Media Forms and Purposes

People use various media forms to *inform*, *persuade*, or *entertain* an audience. What purpose or purposes do you see in the examples below? Write your ideas in the right column.

Media Form	Purpose or Purposes
Newspaper classified ad to sell a used car	
Website for a charity that helps abused and abandoned pets	
Public service announcement about ways to save energy	
Movie trailer for a movie that will soon be released	
Blog about the daily experiences of someone travelling around the world in a sailboat	
A baseball cap with the name of a company that makes sports clothing and equipment	

Media Word Search

E	L	I	T	E	L	E	V	I	S	I	O	N	P
O	P	C	O	M	I	C	M	S	B	P	H	O	R
D	O	P	L	S	E	N	R	O	A	G	S	F	N
V	D	B	A	C	B	I	T	I	V	T	U	L	E
I	C	I	L	L	G	R	W	E	E	I	P	Y	W
D	A	L	S	O	L	A	O	R	R	O	E	E	S
E	S	L	P	L	G	D	M	C	B	N	E	R	P
O	T	B	E	L	D	I	E	S	H	D	E	C	A
G	C	O	E	B	O	O	N	B	A	U	E	T	P
A	O	A	C	W	H	G	U	E	C	R	R	A	E
M	E	R	H	G	R	B	O	O	K	W	T	E	R
E	A	D	V	E	R	T	I	S	E	M	E	N	T
P	O	P	H	O	T	O	G	R	A	P	H	B	L

Word List

comic	brochure	speech	billboard
television	blog	poster	logo
Internet	book	radio	podcast
art	newspaper	videogame	photograph
flyer	movie	menu	advertisement

Media-in-a-Day Tally

Carefully record the examples of media you see, watch, or listen to in one day. Share your results with the class and compare.

Media	Tally
Television	
Radio	
Internet	
Books	
Newspaper	
Flyer	
Brochure	
Comic	
Blog	
Movie	
Music	
Poster	
Billboard	
Logo	
Menu	
Other	

Look at the results. What do you think of your results?

_____

_____

_____

Media Literacy

Background Information

Definitions of *media literacy* vary widely and often include the following abilities:

- To understand and interpret media texts
- To identify a variety of media forms
- To recognize techniques used in media texts and understand the impacts of these techniques
- To communicate effectively using a variety of media forms

Critical thinking skills are a key part of media literacy. Students learn to become critical media "consumers" and effective media creators by actively questioning media texts. Students will also understand the influence media texts have on various individuals and groups, as well as society.

Materials

Blackline Masters

BLM 6: Why Is It Important to Learn About Media? (pp. 17–20)

BLM 7: My Experiences Learning About Media (p. 21)

Assessing Background Knowledge

Most students who have attended school have had previous experiences with media literacy education.

1. Ask students, "How many of you have learned about media in earlier grades?" Ask students who have received media literacy education the following questions and record their responses on the board:

   - What are some of the things you have learned about media?
   - Do you think it is important to learn about media? Why or why not?
   - In what ways can learning about media be helpful to you?

2. Have students read and complete **BLM 6: Why Is It Important to Learn About Media?**

3. Revisit with students the questions asked above and their responses. Ask, "Now that you have completed BLM 6, are there any ideas you think we should add or revise?"

Assessing Students' Attitudes About Media Literacy

1. Use **BLM 7: My Experiences Learning About Media** to gain greater understanding of students' attitudes toward media literacy education. If many of your students do not have a positive attitude toward learning about media, examine the reasons they gave in their responses to question 1. Identify ways to make media literacy a more engaging topic for these students.

2. Review students' responses and use a classroom discussion to identify any issues that you would like to explore in greater depth. Depending on students' responses, you might wish to include the following topics in the discussion:

   - Ask students, "What are your suggestions for more interesting and enjoyable ways to learn about media?"
   - Discuss with students how analyzing and creating media texts are activities that reinforce each other. For example, analyzing what makes a media text effective can give students ideas about how to create effective media texts of their own. Understanding the decisions they make while creating their own media texts can help students analyze media texts created by others.

- Share with students some of the responses to question 3 on BLM 7. Through discussion, clarify any difficulties students have encountered when learning about media. Make notes during the discussion so you can provide instruction in areas where students have encountered difficulties.

Consolidating and Extending Learning

Integrate Media Literacy into Other Subject Areas

To help students understand how media literacy is relevant to them, consider integrating a media literacy perspective into your instruction on other subject areas. For example,

- At the beginning of a lesson in another subject area, take a few moments to examine with students the textbook they are using. Have students identify features of the book or the chapter they are reading, and briefly discuss the purpose of each feature and how each feature is designed to support students' learning.
- When students are watching an instructional video, pause it at two or three places such as a close-up shot, title screen, or an angled shot taken from above or below. At each pause, discuss with students the technique and convention used and what purpose it serves.

Chalkboard Publishing © 2012

Why Is It Important to Learn About Media?

All media try to persuade or influence us on some level. This is why it is important for us to analyze and be critical of media. We need to think about the information and how it is presented to us before we decide what we think, feel, and say about it.

Should We Believe the Media Message?

How do we decide for ourselves whether we should believe a media message? We have to think very carefully about the message and ask ourselves questions about it. For example, imagine you saw a website that said, "Send us $5 and we will send you $50. This is not a hoax!" You might ask yourself these questions:

- Why would this website want to give away money?
- If someone really does want to give away money, why do I have to send $5 first?
- Should I believe this is not a hoax just because the website says it is not?

A short time later, you might see on the news that police are looking for the person who ran the website. He collected thousands of dollars from people who sent in money, but those people did not get any money back.

continued next page ☞

Effective Media Messages

Another good reason to learn about media is to understand how to create an effective media message that achieves its purposes. Imagine that you want to create a poster to advertise a fundraising event at your school. You might look at similar types of posters to see which ones stand out as great examples. Here are some questions you might ask yourself:

Community Cleanup

Help clean up our park!
Friday, June 6, from 2 to 4.
Bring bags to put garbage in.

- Which posters really grab my attention? How do they do that?
- Which posters make me want to go the event? How do they do that?
- Which posters give just enough information? Which posters have too much text?

When you learn what makes a media message effective, you can use this information to make sure your own media messages are effective.

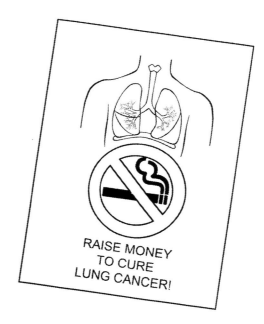

RAISE MONEY
TO CURE
LUNG CANCER!

Brain Stretch

How do you think the media influences young people? Explain your thinking on a separate piece of paper, using information from the reading and your own ideas.

Why Is It Important to Learn About Media?

A value is a belief about what is good or bad or important. Here are some examples:

- It is good to be honest.
- It is important to be loyal to friends.
- Hurting other people's feelings is bad.
- It is important to help others.

1. An advertisement for a new type of jeans says, "Nothing is more important than being popular. Our new jeans will make you the most popular person in your class!"

   a) What value does this advertisement want young people to believe in? Explain your thinking.

   _____

   _____

   b) What does this ad want young people to do?

   _____

   _____

   c) Look at your answer to the question above. How does the ad try to persuade young people to do this?

   _____

   _____

   d) Think carefully about what the ad says. What are two questions you would ask yourself about the ad's messages?

   _____

   _____

   _____

continued next page ☞

2. Think of a television commercial that you enjoy watching. List two or three things about the commercial that made you like it.

_____

_____

_____

_____

_____

_____

_____

_____

_____

3. In your opinion, how can learning about media be useful in your daily life?

_____

_____

_____

_____

_____

_____

_____

_____

_____

My Experiences Learning About Media

1. Put a check mark in the box beside the answer that best describes you.

   In the past, how have you felt about learning about media?
   - ❏ I really enjoyed learning about media.
   - ❏ I thought learning about media was okay, but I did not love it.
   - ❏ I did not enjoy learning about media.

   Give reasons for the answer you chose above.

   _____

   _____

   _____

   _____

2. Which do you enjoy more—analyzing media texts others have created, or creating your own media texts? Explain why.

   _____

   _____

   _____

   _____

3. Think about what you learned about media last year. What topics or ideas were difficult for you to understand? What topics or ideas were easy for you?

   _____

   _____

   _____

   _____

Purpose, Form, and Audience

Background Information

The purpose, form, and audience of a media text are interrelated. Every media text is created for one or more purposes and with some type of audience in mind. The target audience might be general (such as any adult), or specific (such as children between ages 8 and 12 who have a specific interest).

A form is chosen to suit the purpose, but the target audience may also influence the choice of form. For example, forms that rely mainly on visuals are more appropriate for a target audience of young children than forms that rely mainly on text. The audience affects the purpose, because the purpose must be appropriate for the intended audience.

Materials

Samples of various media forms

Blackline Masters

BLM 8: Media Purposes (pp. 26–28)

BLM 9: Media Forms (pp. 29–31)

BLM 10: The Target Audience (pp. 32–34)

BLM 11: Purpose, Form, and Target Audience (p. 35)

Understanding Purpose

1. Ask students to individually brainstorm a list of different ways they have communicated with others during the past week. Use prompts such as the following to get students started:

   - What are some examples of work that you have handed in?
   - Have you emailed or texted a friend?
   - Have you posted a comment on a website?
   - Have you written a note to someone?
   - Have you created a visual, such as a photograph, a diagram, or an illustration?

2. Have students choose specific examples such as completing a quiz in class, texting a message to friend, taking a photograph of a pet doing something funny and sending it to someone. For each example, ask students to identify the reason for the communication. Establish with students that the reason for each communication is also its purpose. The purpose of the quiz is to let the teacher know what the student has learned. The purpose of a text to a friend might be for arranging to meet them at a specific place and time. The purpose of taking the funny photograph of a pet might be to entertain family and friends. Confirm that every media text has a purpose.

3. Have students read and complete **BLM 8: Media Purposes**.

Investigating Media Texts

1. Once again, gather together samples of a variety of media texts such as

   - a sale flyer for a local store
   - a full-page ad from a magazine
   - a music CD
   - a poster (you may be able to borrow one from the school hallways)
   - a nonfiction book

2. Display items one at a time to students and ask, "What is this?" When necessary, rephrase students' responses to focus on the form. For example, if a student says, "That is an ad for cereal," respond with, "Yes, this is an example of a print ad." After students have responded to all the items, confirm with them that they have been identifying media texts.

3. Help students realize that they identify a media form by its characteristics. The following are examples of questions you can ask. Modify the questions according to the media forms you provided. Display the relevant media examples as you ask each question.

- What clues tell you that this is a sale flyer?
- How do you know this is a print ad rather than part of a magazine article?
- How do you know that this nonfiction book is not a novel?
- What clues tell you that this is a poster rather than a flyer?

4. Confirm with students that the features of different media help us to identify the form of a media text. Have students read and complete **BLM 9: Media Forms.**

Thinking About Audience

1. Discuss with students how every media text is created with an audience in mind, and that this audience may be large or small. For example, a telephone directory is created for a very large audience (anyone who uses a phone). But when a student writes a sticky note that says "Remember math test on Thursday," this media text has a very small audience. It is just for the person who wrote the note.

2. Direct students' attention to the media examples you gathered earlier. Hold up each item one at a time and ask, "For what audience was this media text created?" Guide students to be specific in their responses. For example,

- A student says a pop music CD was created for an audience of anyone who likes music. Ask, "Do you think this CD was created for children under the age of five? Was this CD created for people who like only country music?"
- A students says a magazine ad is for people who are interested in buying the product advertised. Ask, "Who would be interested in buying this product? Would this product appeal more to females than males? Would it appeal to people of all ages? Would this product present concerns for, or particularly interest, specific groups of people?"

3. Have students read and complete **BLM 10: The Target Audience.**

4. Ask students to look again at the media samples you have provided. Assist them in identifying conventions associated with each form. For example, students might identify the following conventions of a music CD:

- It comes in a clear plastic case.
- A paper insert in the front of the case is the album cover. Some inserts are in the form of

Chalkboard Publishing © 2012

a booklet that contains such things as song lyrics, photographs of the artist, and credits for people involved with the production of the CD.

- The artist's name and album title are printed on the top of the CD.
- The title of each song (and often the length) is listed on a paper insert in the back of the plastic case.

Consolidating and Extending Learning

Connecting Source and Purpose

Tell students that when they consider the purpose of a media text, they should ask themselves, "Who created this text, or paid for it to be created, and why?" Explain that understanding the source of the text can help them identify its purpose or purposes. For example, you might present to students the following scenario: *You are handed a flyer with the title "Five Reasons to Eat Fresh Fruit."* Ask questions such as the following:

- What are some possible purposes of the flyer?
- If you see that the flyer was created by a group called the Fruit Farmers Association of Canada, what does this tell you about the main purpose of the flyer?
- If you see that the flyer was created by a group called Doctors for Healthy Nutrition, what does this tell you about the flyer's main purpose?
- Who do you think paid for the creation of the flyer?

Identifying Purpose, Form, and Target Audience

Provide students with frequent opportunities to practise identifying the purpose, form, and target audience of a variety of media texts. Students can use **BLM 11: Purpose, Form, and Target Audience** to note clues that help them identify why a media text was created, the form used to present the message, and the target audience for the media text.

Media Purposes

Every media text has a purpose. People create media texts to do, or achieve, something. The following are three common purposes of media texts.

Inform

Some media texts are created to inform people—to provide them with information. A familiar example is a newspaper, which informs people about what is happening in their local community, their country, and the world. A television news broadcast also has the purpose of providing people with information. Here are some other examples of media texts that are created to inform:

- A brochure about the importance of having a healthy diet
- A website video that gives instructions for how to do something
- A nonfiction book about traditions in a variety of cultures

Persuade

Many media texts have the purpose of persuading people to do something, such as buy a particular product or give money to a certain charity. A person who runs for mayor gives speeches to persuade people to vote for him or her. Here are some other examples of media texts that are created to persuade:

- A T-shirt with the message, "Stop cruelty to animals!"
- A public service announcement that encourages people to get a flu shot
- A movie poster that has quotations from positive reviews of the movie

continued next page ☞

Entertain

Many media texts are created to entertain people. Movie trailers, music videos, comic strips, and video games are great examples of media that entertain. They make us laugh, sing, watch, or play.

More Than One Purpose

It is very common for a media text to have more than one purpose. A television commercial might inform you about the health benefits of eating vegetables, then try to persuade you to buy a certain brand of vegetable soup.

Along with informing, persuading, and entertaining, there is another purpose behind many media texts—making money for the people who created the media text. Remember to ask yourself, "Does this media text help someone make money?" or "Who paid for this media text?"

Media Purposes

1. Think about the purposes of each media text below. Put a check mark for each purpose that applies. Be ready to explain your responses.

Media Text	Inform	Persuade	Entertain	Make Money
a) A breakfast cereal commercial that uses funny cartoon characters to tell people what vitamins are in the cereal and why it is important to eat breakfast				
b) A new album from your favourite singer				
c) A school report card				
d) A flyer showing products on sale at a grocery store				
e) A math textbook				
f) A stop sign				
g) A text message inviting you to a birthday party and giving you directions to the house where the party will be held				
h) A television commercial for a new type of running shoes that shows a boy doing amazing skateboard tricks				
i) A poster about a lost puppy and a reward for returning the puppy				
j) A sign that says, "No Parking. Parked cars will be towed away."				

Media Forms

Media texts are created using different forms. For example, if you want to advertise a product, you might use one of the following forms: a television commercial, flyer, poster, or billboard. If you want to tell people about why it is important to protect the environment, you might communicate your message using one of these forms: a book, magazine article, brochure, speech, documentary film, poster, video, or song.

Conventions of Media Forms

You can think about conventions as features or characteristics that are usually part of a certain media form. For example, most novels are written in chapters. Chapters are a convention of the media form of a novel. Cartoons show dialogue inside speech bubbles. Speech bubbles are a convention of cartoons. Here are some examples of conventions of a few media forms:

I wonder if Space Invaders is on tonight?

Media Form	Common Conventions of the Form
Board game	• There is a playing piece for each player. • There is a board with spaces. The playing pieces move from space to space.

continued next page ☞

Television news broadcast 	• There is an anchor person who gives most of the news. • There are video clips showing events in the news. • There are reporters who give details about a news story, often from the place where the event happened.
Blog 	• There is a series of separate entries, which are usually fairly short pieces of text. (In some blogs, each entry is made up of one or more photographs.) • There is usually a date showing when each entry was posted.
Video game 	• There is a goal that the player tries to achieve. • There are different levels, and each level is more difficult than the previous level.

Brain Stretch

Think of one other media forms and list the conventions of the form.

Media Form	Common Conventions of the Form

Media Forms

1. a) Nicola just came back from an amazing trip to Africa. Each day, she wrote in a journal about what she did and saw. Nicola also took many photographs and lots of videos. Now she wants to share her experiences with others. List at least three different media forms she could use.

_____

_____

_____

b) Look at the media forms you listed above. Which form would do the best job of communicating to others information about Nicola's trip? Justify why the form you choose would be better than the others you listed.

_____

_____

_____

_____

2. A television game show is a media form. List at least three conventions that are seen on many television game shows.

_____

_____

_____

3. A wall calendar is a media form. List at least four conventions seen on most wall calendars.

_____

_____

_____

_____

The Target Audience

Media texts are created for an audience—the people who will see or hear the media text. Sometimes the audience is just one person. If you keep a private diary, you are writing for yourself, so you are the audience. Sometimes the audience could include a wide variety of people. A stop sign is a media text that is created for anyone who drives, cycles, or walks on the road.

Many media texts are created for a specific audience, and not for a wide variety of people. We call this type of audience the *target audience,* or sometimes the *intended audience.* For example, if you write a brochure called "How to Take Care of a Pet Rabbit," you are writing for an audience of people who own a pet rabbit or are thinking of getting one. These people are your target audience.

Take a look at these examples of media texts created for a target audience:

Media Text	Target Audience
A commercial for shampoo that is made for long hair	People with long hair
A magazine article called "Ten Ways to Become a Better Basketball Player"	People who play basketball
A website listing stores that give special discounts to senior citizens	Senior citizens
A colouring book that has pictures of female characters from fairy tales	Young girls

continued next page ☞

Creating Media Texts for a Target Audience

When you create a media text, it is important to consider who your target audience is. For example, if you are creating a storybook for young children, you will want to make sure that you do not use words that children will not understand. Young children like to look at pictures in books, so it would be a good idea to include lots of pictures.

Advertisers

Advertisers work hard to create print ads and television commercials that will catch the attention of the people who might buy their product. Advertisers have learned that women grocery shop for the family more often than men do, so women choose what type of laundry detergent to buy. Have you noticed that commercials for laundry detergent almost always feature women? Most advertisers believe that women will pay more attention to a laundry detergent commercial that has a woman as the main character.

Brain Stretch

Fold a large piece of paper in half. One one side, cut out and glue examples of ads for which the target audience is young people. On the other side, cut out and glue examples of ads for which the target audience is adults. Write about the ways they are same and the ways they are different. Contrast other target audiences such as cat owners and dog owners.

The Target Audience

1. Think of a commercial you have seen many times.

a) What type of product or service is the commercial about?

_____

b) Describe the target audience for the commercial.

_____

c) Explain the clues that helped you identify the target audience. (Consider the product or service, and what is shown in the commercial.)

_____

_____

_____

_____

2. Describe the target audience for each of the following media texts. For some examples, you might identify more than one target audience.

a) A class newsletter: _____

b) A song you sing for a talent contest: _____

c) An invitation to your birthday party: _____

d) A poster for a fundraising bake sale at your school:

_____

e) A brochure called "Ten Vegetables You Can Grow in Your Garden"

_____

f) The label on a bottle of cough syrup for young children

_____

Purpose, Form, and Target Audience

Use this page when you are identifying the purpose, form, and target audience of a media text.

Purpose or purposes
Clues that helped me identify the purpose or purposes:

Form
Clues (or conventions) that helped me identify the form:

Target Audience
Clues that helped me identify the target audience:

Print Media

Background Information

Print media: This term is sometimes defined as any media text that is produced on paper, often through the use of a printing press. However, there are many other examples of print media, including a transparency, a blimp with a company logo, and texts that are handwritten or printed from a computer. A print media text does not always contain words. For example, a photograph printed on paper is a print media text.

Materials

Blackline Masters

BLM 12: Print Media (pp. 39–41)

BLM 13: Features in a Print Text (p. 42)

Graphic Organizers

GO 1: A Web Organizer About... (p. 110)

GO 2: Writing Planner (p. 111)

Introducing the Topic

1. Tell students that much of the media that we encounter every day falls into a category called *print media*. On the board or on chart paper, create a two-column chart with the headings "Print Media" and "Non-Print Media." Ask, "What are some examples of print media?" Record students' suggestions in the appropriate column of the chart. If students suggest ideas that are not print media, simply say "No, that is not an example of print media, so I will record it in this column." At this point, do not provide any additional explanation.

2. Students might offer more examples of print media than of non-print media. Encourage students to offer examples by asking, "What are some examples that we could record in the 'Non-Print Media' column?" Add appropriate examples to the chart.

3. Say to students, "Think about the examples we have recorded in each column of the chart. Use these examples to write a definition of the term *print media*." You may wish to have students conduct this part of the activity in pairs or small groups.

4. Invite several individuals, pairs, or small groups to share the definition they developed. Have students decide on a class definition, with guidance from you when required. If necessary, guide students to revise their definition by asking questions such as the following: "Is a letter that you write by hand an example of print media? When is a photograph an example of print media?"

Examining the History and Future of Print Media

1. Explain to students that 100 years ago, most of the media that people encountered were examples of print media. Invite them to offer examples of print media that were available 100 years ago.

2. Tell students that some forms of print media are used less often today than they were 100 years ago. Invite them to offer ideas to explain why this is so. If students have difficulty offering explanations, provide an example such as the following: *Writing a letter was a common way for people to keep in touch 100 years ago. Why do you think people do not write letters as often today?*

3. Have students read and complete **BLM 12: Print Media**.

Creating Print Media Webs

Students could use the additional graphic organizers in various ways to represent information about print media. For example, students could create a web to show the following:

- the conventions associated with a particular form of print media
- examples of print media that are most important in their lives

Consolidating and Extending Learning

Investigating Print Texts

Arrange students in small groups and assign to each group one print text. Have each group use **BLM 13: Features in a Print Text** to note the features and conventions found in the text, and to explain how each one helps the reader. Students might consider print media examples such as a textbook, dictionary, comic book, brochure, etc.

More Ideas

Exploring Picture Books: Discuss with students how pictures and fonts help tell the story and establish the mood of a picture book. Explain that these choices were made by the author and illustrator. Here are some discussion starters:

- How do you feel when you look at this picture? Explain why.
- What has the illustrator done to make you feel this way?
- What colours seem important in this picture? Why do they seem important?
- How do the colours in this picture make you feel? Explain why.

Newspaper Scavenger Hunt: A class scavenger hunt is a great way to explore the content of a newspaper and its features. For example,

- Find the headline.
- Find the dateline.
- What is the editorial about?
- Find a statement of fact.
- Find a statement of opinion.
- Find an editor.
- Find the comics section.
- Name an article in the sports section.
- Name all of the sections of the newspaper.
- Name a byline.
- Find an advertisement.
- Find the weather forecast.
- What news article interests you to read? Why?

Print Text Scrapbook: Have students create a mini-scrapbook that contains five or six examples of different forms of print media, such as a postcard, business card, recipe, brochure, and a cash register receipt. With each example, students note the purpose, form, and target audience, as well as any conventions or features found in the example.

Chalkboard Publishing © 2012

Print Media

Print media is a category that includes all media texts that are printed on paper.

Examples of Print Media

- newspaper
- magazine
- flyer
- restaurant menu
- book
- printed photograph
- greeting card
- billboard
- brochure
- wall calendar
- invitation

A Short History of Print Media

Long ago, books and other printed materials were created by hand. Imagine how long it took to create one copy of a book by writing it all out by hand! People who created copies of written material by hand were called *scribes*. At that time, books were very expensive and only rich people could afford to buy them.

Later, when people began to use the printing press, books and other written materials could be produced in large numbers very quickly and at a much lower cost. Thanks to the printing press, media texts such as newspapers and magazines were invented and quickly became popular.

continued next page ☞

The Future of Print Media

The invention of computers and the Internet has had a big effect on the world of print media. Many people now prefer to read their favourite newspaper or magazine on a website. More and more people now buy ebooks rather than books printed on paper. People can even have their telephone bill and bank statement emailed to them, rather than receiving a printed paper copy in the mail.

Some people say that many types of print media will soon disappear. Will print media texts such as books and magazines soon be available only on devices such as laptops, cell phones, and tablet computers? Will bookstores and magazine stands become a thing of the past? Only time will tell.

Try It!

Ask people how much time each day they spend reading texts printed on paper, and how much time they spend reading texts on a digital device. Share and discuss your survey results with the class.

Print Media

1. List at least four forms of print media that are not listed in the article.

_____

_____

_____

_____

2. What forms of print media have you created? Include examples from schoolwork and any examples from outside school.

_____

_____

_____

3. Some billboards are covered with small lights. Certain lights are lit to create words and pictures. Is this type of billboard an example of print media? Why or why not?

_____

_____

_____

4. How would you feel if paper books were no longer available, and you could read only ebooks? Explain why.

_____

_____

_____

_____

Features in a Print Text

Use this page to identify the features you find in a print text, and explain how each feature helps readers.

Print text: _____

Feature	How the Feature Helps Readers

Digital Media

Background Information

Digital media: Electronic devices and media platforms on which people can create and store media texts, and interact with other people, the device, or the actual application. Digital media includes computers, cell phones, digital cameras, the Internet, social networking websites, and video games. Digital media texts may include sound, still images, animations, photographs, and video.

Materials

- A classroom computer or access to a computer lab
- 3 or 4 pre-selected websites for students to analyze

Blackline Masters

BLM 14: Digital Media (pp. 47–49)

BLM 15: Print Media vs Digital Media (p. 50)

BLM 16: Website Review (pp. 51–52)

BLM 17: Websites I Recommend (p. 53)

BLM 18: Digital Media Savvy Survey (pp. 54–55)

BLM 19: Opinion—Digital Media and Children (pp. 56–57)

BLM 20: Stay Safe on the Internet (pp. 58–60)

BLM 21: Digital Media—Prompts (p. 61)

Introducing the Topic

1. Most students will be aware of several forms of digital media, but they may not be familiar with the term *digital media*. You many wish to explain to students that computer devices store information as digits (usually 1 or 0), and that everything from text to photographs and video games is stored using these digits. Point out that the use of digits to store information on computer devices led to the term *digital media*.

2. Make clear to students that one of the biggest differences between print media and digital media is that digital media gives people the platform to create, share, and communicate their thoughts and ideas. When people read print, they only receive the media messages. On the other hand, digital media largely allows for opportunities to react to media messages. For instance, people can share their ideas via digital media such as social networks, instant messaging, blogs, texting, or uploading videos and photographs.

3. As a class, brainstorm a list of digital media devices that are commonly used today such as laptops, mobile phones, tablets, touchscreen music players, etc. If necessary, prompt students to include devices used to store digital media, such as external hard drives, flash drives, portable music players, CDs, and DVDs.

4. Review with students the list of digital devices created in the last activity. If students have created an extensive list, choose a few items to focus on. For each item, ask the following questions:

   - Does this device create digital media? Does it play or display digital media? Does it store digital media?
   - What media forms do you associate with this device?
   - In what way can you share your ideas with other people using this device?

5. Have students read and complete **BLM 14: Digital Media**.

Transferring Learning

To help students understand that much of what they have learned about print media also applies to digital media, consider having pairs or small groups discuss the question, "In what ways are print media and digital media similar?" Have students list their ideas to share in a class discussion. Students might offer ideas such as the following:

- Many media texts available in print are also available in digital form (for example, novels, photographs, ads, newspapers, magazines).

- Many of the conventions and features of print media are seen in the comparable digital form (for example, a print novel and a novel in ebook form are both divided into chapters).
- All media texts, whether print or digital, have a purpose, form, and target audience.

Analyzing Websites

The Internet is full of free information, photographs, and videos just a few clicks away. Discuss with students the importance of sifting through and evaluating websites. Since most students will be familiar with various types of websites, you might use them as a starting point for analyzing digital media.

1. Before engaging students in this activity, select and bookmark three or four different types of websites to use as examples. Be sure to preview websites before showing them to students. Possible examples include the following:

   - a news website
   - a music website
   - a blog website
   - a school website
   - a forum (for example, there are many forums that provide help to people with computer problems)
   - an information website

2. Briefly guide students through the homepage of each website, asking questions such as the following:

   - Does the website offer any information or clues about who created it? What purpose or purposes does the website have?
   - How does the website make use of visual elements, such as colour (for print elements and backgrounds), photographs, diagrams, and illustrations?
   - Which form of media is used most to express the messages on this website: visuals, animations, sounds, or text?
   - What common conventions of websites do we see on this website? (For example, a navigation menu, photographs or other visuals that can be clicked to view larger, hyperlinks, links to sites on a related topic.)
   - Who do you think is the target audience for this website? What are the clues?
   - From what you have seen, does this appear to be a good website? Can you think of any ways to improve this website?

3. Ask students to use **BLM 15: Print Media vs Digital Media** to keep track of their print media and digital media use for one day. The next day, invite students to share their results. List their answers on the board or chart paper. Take a tally of how many students used each type of media. Identify and discuss any trends as a class.

4. Assign student pairs to use **BLM 16: Website Review** to review a website from an approved list compiled by the teacher. Once the reviews are complete, have students share the results and ask them to explain their reasoning.

5. Ask students to complete **BLM 17: Websites I Recommend.** Invite students to share their results. Examine any trends as a class.

6. Have students complete **BLM 18: Digital Media Savvy Survey** and reflect as a class on the results.

7. Have students read **BLM 19: Opinion—Digital Media and Children.** Ask students to complete the outline. Invite them to share their outline with the class.

8. Have students read **BLM 20: Stay Safe on the Internet.** Discuss each section as a class. Ask students whether they have heard of any other ways to stay safe on the Internet. (Ask them to think about how specialized software helps keep people and computers safe.)

Consolidating and Extending Learning

Discussing or Writing About Digital Media

The questions on **BLM 21: Digital Media—Prompts** can be used in a variety of ways:

- Choose appropriate questions to guide pair, small-group, or class discussions. You might provide students with the questions in advance and ask them to jot their initial responses. Giving students an opportunity to reflect on the questions beforehand can lead to richer discussions, and encourage the participation of students who are often hesitant to participate.
- Allow pairs or small groups to choose the questions that interest them most and use these questions to guide their discussion.
- Choose, or allow students to choose, questions to use as prompts for journal entries.

Imagining Digital Media in the Future

Briefly review with students some of the advancements that have taken place in digital media over the past decade or so. (Typing "digital media timeline" into a search engine should bring up some websites that provide useful background information.) Then ask students to imagine what advances in digital media will take place in the next 10 to 15 years. Students could brainstorm ideas in small groups, then share their ideas with the class. As a follow-up, you could ask some students who are interested in digital media to research advancements that are planned or underway. Students could present their findings to the class.

 Chalkboard Publishing © 2012

Digital Media

Digital media includes media texts that can be stored and shared electronically on a computer device (including cell phones and portable music players), a CD, or a DVD. Digital media can be created on electronic devices such as a computer, or a digital camera or camcorder. Digital media includes all media created, produced, and or shared on a digital platform. This includes broadcast media. All television and radio programming is now produced digitally and also is streamed online.

Digital Media Forms

After the Internet was invented, some new media forms began to appear. For example,

Websites: A website is a collection of webpages. A website can focus on one topic, or may contain information about many different topics.

Blogs: A blog can be one section of a website, or a blog may be the only thing on a website. A blog has a series of separate entries (often each entry is dated), and each entry is usually fairly short (often from one paragraph to three or four paragraphs). Most blogs are updated regularly by adding new entries. Some blogs include photographs, while others have just photographs and little or no text. Many blogs are created by individuals who want to share their thoughts, opinions, and interests. These blogs are like online journals.

continued next page ☞

Text Messages: Text messages are usually very short messages. They often contain short forms, such as "u" for "you" and "LOL" for "laughing out loud." People often include emoticons. These are keyboard symbols and punctuation marks used to create faces that express emotions such as :) —a "smiley face" that communicates that the writer is happy or amused.

"Old Media" Becomes Digital Media

You can think of "old media" as media forms that existed before the computer was invented—for example, television shows, movies, songs, radio shows, and various forms of print media. These examples of "old media" become digital media when they are stored and shared on a computer. Television shows and movies can be stored as video files. Songs can be downloaded and stored as music files. Radio shows are available through the Internet as sound files called *podcasts*.

Almost any form of print media can be created and stored on a computer. Information or visuals printed on paper can be scanned to become computer files. Thanks to computer technology, it is quite easy to convert "old media" into digital media.

1. If you have created your own website or blog, tell why you wanted to create it. If you do not have a website or blog, explain why you would or would not want to create one. (If you do not know how to create these digital media forms, assume someone would help you.)

_____

_____

_____

_____

2. Compare your use of "old media" and new media. Write approximately how much time (in hours) you spend in one week doing each of the following.

"Old Media"	Time Spent	Digital Media	Time Spent
Watching television, seeing a movie in a theatre		Watching videos on the Internet, watching movies on a computer or on DVDs	
Listening to music on the radio		Listening to music on CDs and music you have downloaded from the Internet	
Reading print media, such as books and magazines		Reading texts on the Internet (such as websites and blogs), reading ebooks	
Playing board games, doing crosswords, sudoku puzzles, word searches, etc., in print media		Playing video games (on television or computer), and doing crosswords, sudoku puzzles, word searches, etc., online	

Print Media vs Digital Media

For one entire day, keep track of all the ways you use print media and digital media. For example, in the Print Media column you might write "Looked up a word in a print dictionary." In the "Digital Media" column, you might write "Found information on the Internet to help with homework."

Print Media	Digital Media

Website Review

Website address: _____

What is the purpose of the website? Explain your thinking.	❑ Inform ❑ Persuade ❑ Entertain
Does the webpage author list their name and email address?	
Is the website current? Does it have the date updated or revised on it?	
Who is the target audience? Explain the clues.	

continued next page ☞

Is the website easy to navigate?	
Which form of media is used most to express the messages on this website: visuals, animations, sounds, or text?	
Does the website want something? Explain.	
What are the clear and hidden messages on this website?	
Would you recommend this website? Why or why not?	

Websites I Recommend

Website	Purpose of Website	Why I Like the Website

Digital Media Savvy Survey

Take this survey and think about how you keep yourself safe when using digital media.

How I Keep Myself Safe	Always	Sometimes	Never
I do not give out any personal Information such as my name, age, address, or school.			
I only send a cyber pal a picture of myself after checking with my parent or guardian.			
I only arrange a face-to-face meeting with a cyber pal after checking with my parent or guardian.			
I tell my parent or guardian right away if I come across any information that makes me feel uncomfortable.			
I do not respond to any messages that are mean or in any way make me feel uncomfortable. If I receive that type of message, I tell my parent or guardian immediately.			
I do not add or accept friend requests from people that I do not know.			

continued next page ☞

I do not give out my passwords to anyone (even close friends) other than my parent or guardian.			
I am a good online citizen and do not do anything that bullies people or is against the law.			
I am careful to check with my parent or guardian before downloading or installing software, or doing anything that might harm our computer or mobile device or jeopardize my family's privacy.			

Look at your responses. How safe do you think you are when online? Explain your thinking.

_____

_____

_____

_____

_____

_____

_____

Did You Know?

Netiquette: Rules of behaviour or etiquette that apply when using computer networks, especially the Internet.

Social networks: Online communities of people who use a website or other technologies to communicate.

Opinion—Digital Media and Children

Digital media is available 24 hours a day, 365 days a year! If given permission, children could post, instant message, upload, download, and text almost any time and anywhere. Some parents or guardians are very strict about what their child can and cannot do.

Do you agree or disagree with these parents? Use this outline to explain your thinking.

Statement of My Opinion

_____

_____

_____

_____

_____

Reason

_____

_____

_____

_____

_____

continued next page ☞

Supporting Details

_____
_____
_____
_____
_____

Reason

_____
_____
_____
_____

Supporting Details

_____
_____
_____
_____

Restate Your Opinion

_____
_____
_____
_____
_____

Stay Safe on the Internet

The Internet is an amazing resource. Many people say that they would have a difficult time living without access to the Internet. Do you know how to stay safe online? Here are a few tips.

Social Networking and Instant Messaging

Social networking websites and instant messaging (often called IM) can be great ways to keep in touch with friends. But be careful!

- When you set up a personal profile, you may need to give a lot of information about yourself, such as your name, address, email address, telephone number, and more. This information may become available to other people. Before you set up a profile, get a parent or guardian to help you. Make sure to find out who will have access to your personal information, and whether there are ways to keep this information private. Do not include a photograph of yourself in your profile!

- Do not use social networking websites or IM to connect with people you do not know in real life. If you do meet someone new on the Internet, make sure a parent or guardian knows about it. Never arrange to meet a new Internet friend in person, unless a parent or guardian can go with you.

- Be careful what you say in an instant message or on a social networking website. Your comments can be copied and sent to anyone. You might trust the friend you are communicating with, but what happens if you have an argument with your friend or someone steals your friend's laptop or cell phone?

continued next page ☞

Passwords

Email requires a password. So do many other things people do on the Internet. Keep these password safety tips in mind.

- It is okay to give your passwords to a parent or guardian, but do not share your passwords with anyone else—not even a close friend.

- Choose passwords that are not easy to guess. Create a password from random letters and numbers. You should not use the same password on different websites. So make sure you write down your passwords and keep them in a safe and private place, or give them to a parent or guardian. Change your passwords regularly.

Email

Email might seem to be a safe way to communicate with people, but you still need to be careful.

- Do not choose an email address that has your full name. Avoid choosing an email address that allows people to guess your full name.

- Remember that an email you send can be forwarded to other people—so be careful what you say.

- Spam is email that is sent to thousands of people who did not ask to receive it. Spam can be dangerous and can contain viruses that harm your computer. People who want to trick you into giving out your personal information can send it. Before you open an email, check to see who sent it. If you do not know the person, delete the email without opening it.

- If you are getting a lot of spam, ask a parent or guardian to help you learn what you can do about the problem. Remember that if a website asks for your email address before you play a game or do a survey, someone will probably send you spam.

continued next page ☞

Beware of Bullies—and Do Not Be One!

Bullies who use the Internet to hurt people's feelings are a serious problem.

- If you use the Internet to bully people, you can get into serious trouble! Whether you are online or offline, remember this rule: "Treat others the way you would like them to treat you."

- If someone bullies you—on or off the Internet—be sure to tell a parent or guardian. If anyone sends you an email, attachment, text message, or a website link that makes you feel uncomfortable, always tell a parent or guardian.

Learn More About Internet Safety

The tips on these pages are just a start. Here are some ways to learn more:

- Type "Internet safety for kids" into a search engine. There are many websites that will give you more information.

- Talk with a parent or guardian about Internet safety. Remember to always let a parent or guardian know what you are doing online.

Brain Stretch

On a separate piece of paper, draft a public service announcement that gives Internet safety tips for children. When you are finished, share it with your class. Use this checklist to help you.

❑ My public service announcement has a clear message about Internet safety for children.

❑ My public service announcement is 15 to 30 seconds long.

❑ I created my public service announcement to appeal to my target audience. (children or adults)

❑ I practised reading my public service announcement with expression.

Digital Media—Prompts

Use the following prompts to prepare for a discussion, guide a discussion, or to give you ideas for a journal entry. On a separate piece of paper, you can jot some quick ideas to help you get started.

1. In what ways does digital media make your life easier? (Consider digital media texts that you create, as well of forms of digital media that you read, watch, or listen to.)

2. How important is the Internet in your daily life? What would you miss most about the Internet if you no longer had access to it? Why?

3. Some people have careers that involve creating digital media, such as website creators, video game creators, and graphic designers. Would a career as a digital media creator interest you? Why or why not?

4. What are some of the disadvantages of digital media? (For example, digital media makes it easy to "fake" or alter a photograph and pass it off as real.) Consider the disadvantages of various forms of digital media.

Deconstructing Media Messages

Background Information

To fully understand what a media text communicates, students need to be able to interpret clear messages (messages clearly stated in the text) and hidden messages (messages that are implied). Students also need to be able to identify values (beliefs about what is important in life) that are communicated in a media text, and to decide whether they share those values. By becoming aware of the persuasive techniques used in media texts, students learn to see how some media texts seek to manipulate their audience.

Materials

- Several magazines that contain many ads
- Recorded samples of commercial clips, television shows, public service announcements, etc.
- Product packaging samples

Blackline Masters

BLM 22: Fact or Opinion? (p. 69)

BLM 23: Identifying Values in the Media (p. 70)

BLM 24: Persuasive Techniques (pp. 71–74)

BLM 25: Media Messages—Prompts (p. 75)

BLM 26: Commercial Analysis (p. 76)

BLM 27: Stereotypes (pp. 77–80)

Teacher Tips

- Try to keep the segments short when showing commercial clips, television show samples, public service announcements, etc. This will encourage students to stay focused.
- Turn off the sound when specifically examining media images.
- Cover the screen when specifically examining sounds and sound effects.
- Remember that students will understand and interpret media messages differently. There is no "right" way to interpret a media text. Validate opinions.

　　　　　　　　　　　　　　　　　　　　　Chalkboard Publishing © 2012

Identifying Facts and Opinions

1. Discuss with students the difference between a fact (a piece of information that is generally known to be true or has been proven to be true) and an opinion (a personal view or judgment which may or may not be based on facts). Point out that sometimes opinions are easy to identify because they contain words such as "I think," "I believe," and "in my opinion."

2. Explain that people sometimes state opinions as though they were facts; for example, "Spring is the best season of the year." Present students with some statements and ask them to decide which are facts and which are opinions. Possible examples include the following:

   - Dogs make better pets than cats. *(opinion)*
   - In Canada, summer is the warmest season of the year. *(fact)*
   - A movie based on a book is never as good as the book. *(opinion)*
   - Reading an ebook is more enjoyable than reading a book printed on paper. *(opinion)*
   - On most television stations, shows are interrupted by commercials. *(fact)*

3. Provide opportunities such as the following for students to distinguish between facts and opinions within a variety of media texts.

   Print Media: Arrange students in pairs or small groups. Distribute to each group some magazines, newspapers, flyers, etc. Instruct students to find statements they would label as fact or opinion. All members of the group should agree on the decisions. Encourage students to look through articles, as well as advertisements. Have students record their findings on **BLM 22: Fact or Opinion?**

   Provide time for each pair or group to share some examples of facts and opinions they found. When students offer examples of opinions, ask, "Is that opinion clearly presented as an opinion, or is it presented in a way that makes it sound as though it is a fact?" Ask students, "Why might the advertiser want to present an opinion as a fact?" Through discussion, elicit that presenting an opinion as a fact is a persuasive technique that advertisers sometimes use to help the ad achieve its purpose. In addition, discuss the appropriateness of the use of opinions as students mention examples of opinions in articles.

News Broadcasts: As a class, watch an age-appropriate television news story prerecorded by the teacher. Discuss the following:

- What is this news story about?
- Whose point of view do we hear?
- Whose point of view is missing?
  - How would another point of view change the story?
  - What is fact?
  - What is opinion? How do you know?

Websites: Ask students how they decide which websites are good to use for research projects to get other information they need. Record their answers on the board. Possible answers:

- I would use the website recommended to me by my teacher, friend, etc.
- I would the first website that comes up on the results page after doing a keyword search.

Then discuss how they know that the website is credible.

Blogs: Ask students the purpose of blogs. A *blog* is a website that lets people contribute their ideas, comments, and opinions about various topics in a journal format. Show some examples of blogs and have students complete **BLM 22: Fact or Opinion?**

Identifying Values

1. Establish with students that a *value* is a personal view or judgment about what is important in life. Provide two or three examples of familiar sayings that communicate a value. Ask students to write a statement about the value beginning with "It is important…". For example,

   - Honesty is the best policy. (It is important to be honest.)
   - Treat others the way you would like them to treat you. (It is important to treat others with kindness and consideration.)
   - All things come to those who wait. (It is important to be patient.)

2. Explain to students that media texts sometimes communicate values without clearly stating them. Provide students with the following ad message and ask them to identify the value it communicates:

   Do not embarrass yourself by wearing last year's fashions! At Fred's Fashion Store, you will find all the latest fashions. (Value: It is important to always wear the latest fashions.)

Then ask questions such as the following:

- Do you think everyone agrees with this value?
- Why would Fred's Fashion Store want to encourage people to believe in this value? How does this value help the ad to achieve its purpose?

3. Confirm with students that media texts can promote certain values to achieve the purpose of the text. Discuss why it is important for people to decide for themselves whether they accept values presented in media texts.

4. To help students understand that many different types of media texts can communicate values, you might choose use one or more of the following activities:

- Discuss with students the values communicated in fiction texts. You might start by reading aloud some short fables with morals. Before you read and discuss the value presented in the moral, ask students what value is presented in the text. As a follow-up, ask students to identify the values communicated in any appropriate stories the class has read recently.

- From the magazines you have gathered, select some examples of ads that communicate a value and ask students to identify the value. Discuss why the advertiser would choose to communicate that value.

- Ask students to choose a cause that is important to them (such as preventing cruelty to animals, preventing bullying, or saving endangered animals). Ask them to identify one value they hold that makes this cause meaningful to them. Students could then create a short media message about the cause that communicates the value they identified.

- As a class, brainstorm a list of different types of television genres such as reality shows, nature shows, news programs, sitcoms, educational programs, cartoons, etc. Then identify the values usually associated with each television genre and example of a show. Encourage students to explain their thinking.

- Have students examine a variety of media texts such as a television show from a particular genre, public service announcement, print advertisement, or music. Ask them to complete the **BLM 23: Identifying Values in the Media**. Discuss as a class how media texts may influence students' values.

Understanding Clear and Hidden Messages

1. Explain to students that every media form has a message.

- A *clear message* is one that is obviously stated. It is easy to understand the message in the media text quickly.
- A *hidden message* is one that is suggested, or communicated without being clearly stated. You have to listen to or watch the media text carefully to understand the message.

Provide examples such as the following:

- (Clear message) The cover of a pamphlet has the text "Smoking can kill you."
- (Hidden message) On a televised public service announcement without any words, an image of a cigarette package slowly changes into an image of a coffin.

Discuss with students how the public service announcement communicates the message "Smoking can kill you" without clearly stating this information. Point out that the message is *suggested* through images.

2. Establish with students that hidden messages can be conveyed in a variety of ways. You might use examples such as the following:

- Recall with students the ad message for Fred's Fashion Store (see Identifying Values, step 2, on page 64) and discuss how the value it presents is an implicit message that is communicated through words.
- *A television commercial shows a dog lying on the floor, looking tired and sad. A woman feeds the dog "Doggie Delight" dog food. The next shot shows the dog looking happy and active as it runs after a ball tossed by its owner.* Discuss with students what implicit message is communicated by the visuals in this commercial (your dog will be happier and more active if you feed it this dog food).
- *A radio commercial for an ocean cruise features a popular song played at the beginning, and includes the lyrics "When you sail across the ocean blue, no worries come your way."* Discuss with students what implicit message the song communicates (you will be cheerful and worry-free if you go on our cruise).

3. Ask students to look through the magazines you provided to find ads that communicate clear messages. Have students clearly state the clear message, and explain why the advertiser would want to communicate this message.

4. Invite students to examine various examples of packaging for similar food products such as different brands of soup or cereal. Students may use any of the graphic organizers to show their findings. Once complete, students may share their findings with the class. Prompt students' thinking by asking the following questions:

- What are the similarities and differences in the packaging for a particular type of food?
- What do you like or not like about the packaging?
- Who is the target audience? What are the clues?
- What is the clear message on the packaging?
- What is the hidden message on the packaging?
- Is there a slogan?
- Does the packaging persuade you to want to buy the product and taste the contents? For example, the size of a package is larger than a similar product, but there is a smaller amount of the contents.
- Are there attention-grabbing promotions on the packaging such as free gifts or contests that promise big prizes?

Note: If possible, give students an opportunity to taste different samples of similar products and to give their opinion whether the product looked and tasted as they expected. In addition, ask students whether they noticed the amount of the contents in relation to size of the packaging. Before bringing food into the classroom, check with students to find out whether there are any food allergies or other concerns.

Consolidating and Extending Learning

Exploring Persuasive Techniques in Advertising

As you introduce various commercials and print advertisements, explore with students the ways advertisers try to convince people to buy their product. These techniques may include

- repeated words
- showing kids having fun
- repeated words
- catchy song
- characters kids know
- discounts
- prizes
- catchy phrases
- music

On chart paper, keep track of persuasive techniques so students may refer to them when they create their own advertisements. The list below are words and phrases commonly found in advertising.

- Amazing
- Just arrived
- New and improved!
- Quick
- Announcing
- Last chance!
- First choice!
- Hurry
- At last!
- Be the first!
- Easy
- New
- Before it is too late!
- Introducing
- Recommended by
- Free

Have students read and complete **BLM 24: Persuasive Techniques** to learn about common persuasive techniques.

Discussing or Writing About Media Messages

The questions on **BLM 25: Media Messages—Prompts** can be used in a variety of ways:

- Choose appropriate questions to guide pair, small-group, or class discussions. Provide students with the questions in advance and ask them to jot their initial responses. Giving students an opportunity to reflect on the questions beforehand can lead to richer discussions, and encourage the participation of students who are often hesitant to participate.
- Allow pairs or small groups to choose the questions that interest them most, and use these questions to guide their discussion.
- Choose, or allow students to choose, questions to use as prompts for journal entries.

Creating a Print Media Messages Display

Invite students to contribute print media texts such as ads, brochures, flyers, and letters to the editor to a classroom bulletin board or wall display. Students should choose texts that provide an example of at least one of the following:

- an opinion stated as a fact
- a clear message
- a value
- a persuasive technique

Ask students to post along with the print media text a brief note explaining which of the elements listed above are present, and where each element is present in the text. For example, a student might post with a travel brochure a note such as the following: *The brochure title "Nothing Beats a Vacation in Barbados" presents an opinion as a fact.*

Encourage all students to review the media texts posted to see whether they can identify any additional elements that have not been noted. (You may wish to review all students' contributions before they are posted.)

Analyze a Commercial

Analyze commercials as a class, using **BLM 26: Commercial Analysis.** Alternatively, students could analyze a commercial for homework and share their results with the class.

Examining Stereotypes

Have students read **BLM 27: Stereotypes.** Discuss each section as a class.

Comparing Media Messages

Use the additional graphic organizers found in this resource to compare a variety of media texts and their messages.

Fact or Opinion?

Media text: _____

Purpose of media text: _____

Short description of media text: _____

_____

Look for examples of facts and opinions in the media text you are examining.

Fact	Opinion

Identifying Values in the Media

A *value* is a personal view or judgment about what is important in life.
Here are some examples:

- love of family
- beauty
- competition
- education/knowledge
- helping others
- having fun
- adventure
- justice
- being honest
- good health
- money
- fame

Examine a variety of media texts and identify the values that are displayed.

Media Text Example	Value or Values Displayed	What are the clues?

Persuasive Techniques

Media texts often have the purpose of persuading us to do something, to agree with an opinion, or both. Here are two examples:

Media Form	Message	Persuasion
Television commercial	Our new dish soap works even better than our old dish soap.	**Do something:** Buy the new dish soap.
Radio public service announcement	Getting enough exercise is important to your health.	**Do something:** Get more exercise.

Here are just a few of the ways, or techniques, that media creators use to persuade us:

Present only some of the facts: Facts are great, but is the media text giving you all the facts? A print ad for Soapy laundry detergent may tell you that it is not as expensive as Super Clean detergent, and it may be true. It may also be true that Super Clean works much better than Soapy—but of course the ad does not tell you that.

Present a testimonial: A testimonial is when someone says, "I have used this product and I just love it!" The person who says this may be an actor who was paid to make the commercial. That person may never even have tried the product. Sometimes famous people are paid to do a testimonial.

Trust me! I love this product!

continued next page ☞

Exaggerate: A product may work well, but not as well as the ad claims. An exercise machine may make people stronger. But if an ad suggests that it will give people huge muscles in just two or three weeks, the ad is exaggerating.

Present an expert's opinion: A dentist should be an expert on toothpaste, right? If you see a commercial in which a dentist says, "This is the best toothpaste you can buy," should you believe it? How do you know that nine out of ten dentists actually do think the toothpaste is that great?

Make people afraid: Some ads try to make people afraid that if they do not use a product, something bad or embarrassing will happen. Here is a message that uses this technique: "If you do not use our air freshener, visitors might notice unpleasant odours in your house that you did not even know were there." If you feel afraid this might happen to you, you might buy the product.

Jump on the bandwagon: Some ads want to convince you that you need to join the crowd. The message is "Everyone is buying it/using it/doing it! You should too!"

Persuasive Techniques

1. For each media message below, write the technique of persuasion that is used.

Media Message	Technique of Persuasion
a) Dr. Stevenson says that a new type of pill will keep you from catching colds.	
b) If you do not chew our new gum, you might have bad breath and not know it.	
c) A mom says that her baby likes a certain type of baby food better than any other.	
d) A car ad presents three true facts that should convince you to buy the car.	
e) Use our new floor cleaner and your floors will be shinier than ever before.	
f) A young person says that a new video game is the best one he has ever played.	

continued next page ☞

2. Look at the list of products. Chose a persuasive technique you think would work best with your target audience. Then write the media message that you would use in a commercial to persuade people to buy the product. Be prepared to justify your choice of technique!

Product	Media Message
a) Product: Cereal **Target Audience:** Children **Persuasive Technique:** _____ _____	
b) Product: Gym Membership **Target Audience:** Adults **Persuasive Technique:** _____ _____	
c) Product: Jeans **Target Audience:** Teenagers **Persuasive Technique:** _____ _____	

Media Messages—Prompts

Use the following prompts to prepare for a discussion, guide a discussion, or to give you ideas for a journal entry. On a separate piece of paper, you can jot some quick ideas to help you get started.

1. Do you think that media messages can convince people to believe in certain values? (Consider a variety of media forms such as video games, popular songs, music videos, and ads.) Why or why not?

2. Which techniques of persuasion would most likely convince you to buy a product? Which techniques would not work well with you? For each technique you mention, explain why you would or would not find it convincing.

3. Why do you think that some media texts use hidden messages? Why would these texts not state all messages clearly?

4. Sometimes people buy a product because the ad or commercial convinced them that the product was really good. Then, after buying the product, they find out that it is not nearly as good as they expected it to be. What can you do to prevent this from happening to you?

5. Why do you think manufacturers feature famous people or interesting cartoon characters on the front of a package? Explain your reasoning.

Commercial Analysis

1. What is the purpose of this commercial?

❏ **Inform**   ❏ **Persuade**   ❏ **Entertain**

2. What is the message of the commercial?

_____

_____

3. Who is the target audience? What are the clues?

_____

_____

4. Describe any sound effects or music in the commercial. What do the sound effects or music make you think about?

_____

_____

5. Describe any visual images in the commercial. What do the visual images make you think about?

_____

_____

6. What persuasive techniques are used in the commercial?

❏ Bandwagon   ❏ Exaggeration   ❏ Testimonial   ❏ Fear

❏ Famous People   ❏ Only Some Facts   ❏ Expert Opinion   ❏ Other

Explain how this technique is used:

_____

_____

_____

_____

Stereotypes

What Are Stereotypes?

Stereotypes are common ideas about groups of people. In television shows, movies, and books, we often see stereotypes about males and females. For example, males are strong and do not cry, and females are sensitive and concerned about how they look. When a character in media fits a common stereotype, we say that it is a *stereotypical* character.

What Is the Problem With Stereotypes?

The problem with stereotypes is that when we see them over and over again in media, they can affect how we think about ourselves and others. It is a stereotype that males like sports. If you are a male and you do not like sports, you may think there is something wrong with you because a stereotype says that males are supposed to like sports. Is it reasonable to believe that *all* males should like sports? No, it is not.

It is also a stereotype that females are not very interested in sports. People may think it strange when a girl loves watching sports on television and enjoys playing various sports. There is no reason why a girl should not like sports. People think this is strange only because they believe the stereotype that females are not very interested in sports.

Stereotypes about what males and females are "supposed" to be like are called *gender stereotypes*.

continued next page ☞

Other Types of Stereotypes

Gender stereotypes are just one type of stereotype. There are many other types too. For example, people may have stereotypes about nationalities and cultures. Some people who live outside of Canada believe this stereotype: "Canadians are very polite." You have probably learned that this is not true of all Canadians—some are very polite and some are not. Stereotypes can make us believe that something is true of everyone in a group, even though this is not really the case.

Here are some other stereotypes you may have come across:

- Rich people do not like being around people who do not have lots of money.
- Boys who are really great at sports do not get good marks in school.
- Females who are blonde are not as smart as females with darker hair.

Remember that people are individuals, and each person is unique. Stereotypes can lead us to make assumptions about what we should be like, and what other people are like. Do not fall into that trap! Be the person you want to be. Take the time to learn what people are like as individuals, and do not assume that something is true of everyone in a certain group.

Stereotypes

1. Think of a character in a television show, movie, book, or comic who is an example of a common gender stereotype.

   Name of character: _____

   Title of television show, movie, book, or comic the character is from:

   _____

   Describe a stereotype often used for that type of character:

   _____

   _____

   _____

2. Think of a character in a television show, movie, book, or comic who does not fit into a common gender stereotype.

   Name of character: _____

   Title of television show, movie, book, or comic the character is from:

   _____

   Describe a stereotype often used for that type of character:

   _____

   _____

   _____

   Explain why the character does not fit into the stereotype:

   _____

   _____

   _____

continued next page ☞

3. What is the most important thing you have learned about stereotypes?

_____

_____

_____

_____

_____

_____

_____

_____

4. When we see stereotypes in the media over and over again, those stereotypes can affect how we think and feel about ourselves and others. Do you agree? Explain your thinking.

_____

_____

_____

_____

_____

_____

_____

_____

Creating Media Texts

Background Information

The purpose of media literacy education is to encourage students to become critical "consumers" of media. It helps them learn to discriminate facts from opinions, interpret explicit and implicit messages, understand the values presented in a media texts, and identify any persuasive techniques that are used. However, students also need to learn how to create effective media texts. Analyzing and creating media texts are activities that reinforce each other. Students can apply what they learn from analyzing media texts to creating their own media texts. By creating media texts, students will learn what types of decisions need to be made and make those decisions themselves based on the purpose, form, and target audience. As a result, students improve their ability to deconstruct the media texts they read, view, and listen to.

Materials

Blackline Masters

BLM 28: Media Text Planner (p. 90)

BLM 29: Tips for Creating Media Texts (pp. 91–92)

BLM 30: Media Text Self-Evaluation (p. 93)

BLM 31: Using Colour to Help Sell a Product (pp. 94–95)

BLM 32: Tips for Print Advertisements (p. 96)

BLM 33: Oral Presentation Outline (pp. 97–99)

BLM 34: Write a Review (p. 100)

BLM 35: Magazine Article Checklist (p. 101)

BLM 36: A Letter of Advice (p. 102)

BLM 37: Brilliant Brochure (p. 103)

BLM 38: _____ T-shirt (p. 104)

BLM 39: Design and Sell Your Dream Home (p. 105)

BLM 40: Create a Magazine (pp. 106–107)

BLM 41: Poster Checklist (p. 108)

BLM 42: Create a Board Game (p. 109)

Note: When assigning media creation activities, be sure to provide instruction on the media texts students are asked to use or will choose from. If students are not familiar with the characteristics and conventions of a type of media text, they will have a difficult time using it to create an effective product. In addition, ensure students are able to use any equipment required to produce a media text, such as a video camera and editing software. Avoid situations in which students are spending much of their time figuring out how to use the equipment.

Discussing Purpose, Form, and Target Audience

Emphasize to students that, at all stages of the process, it is very important to keep in mind the purpose, form, and target audience of a media text they are creating. Here are some things students should consider:

During the initial planning process
- Have I identified a clear purpose (or purposes) for my media text before I go any farther?
- Who is my target audience? Do I want to target a very specific audience?
- What forms would work best for my purpose? Are there any forms that would be particularly suitable for my target audience?

After deciding on a purpose, form, and target audience
- What are the conventions of the form I chose? Which of these conventions will help me to achieve my purpose? Are there any conventions that will help make my message clearer to my target audience?
- What techniques will help my media text achieve its purpose(s)? Should I use any techniques of persuasion? Will elements such as colour, visuals, humour, or music work with my form and help appeal to the target audience?

While creating the media text
- Is my media text coming together in the way I thought it would? Do I need to improve any of the conventions to achieve my purpose and appeal to the target audience? Do I need to consider using other conventions?
- Do I feel that my media text will grab the attention of my target audience? Are there additional techniques or elements that I should include?
- Have I organized information in a way that will be clear to my target audience? Have I made the most important information stand out so my target audience will not miss it?

Provide students with **BLM 28: Media Text Planner** and **BLM 29: Tips for Creating Media Texts** to help with the initial planning process. To support students after this initial stage, conduct brief individual conferences as they create their media text.

Sharing and Analyzing Students' Media Texts

Provide time for students to share their media texts with the class. The student who created the media text could ask classmates questions such as the following. This step gives students opportunities to analyze media texts, as well as offer feedback.

- What do you think is the purpose of this media text?
- For a media form, I chose _____. What conventions of this form have I used?
- Who is the target audience?
- What do you think works best in my media text?
- What is one suggestion you would make for improving my media text?

After students have received feedback from classmates, you might have them complete **BLM 30: Media Text Self-Evaluation**.

Extending and Consolidating Learning

Teacher Tips for Creating Media Text Activities

- Model and reinforce required skills. If students are not familiar with the characteristics and conventions of a type of media text, they will have a difficult time using it to create an effective product.
- Make sure there are enough materials for each student, along with a sample of what is expected.
- Have students create media portfolios where they can store their media projects, assignments, and learning logs.

Listening to a Media Expert

Invite into the classroom someone whose profession involves creating media texts. For example, invite a reporter from a local newspaper or television station, a graphic artist, a Web designer, or someone from an advertising agency. Ask the guest to share with students details about their job and, if possible, to share some media texts they were involved in creating. (You might first brief the guest on what students have been learning about media and ask them to touch on some these topics during the presentation.) Provide time for students to ask questions.

Activity Ideas for Creating Media Texts

Class Audio Book

As a class, or in small groups, record an audio version of a picture book. Cast students in roles, and insert sound effects and music to accentuate dramatic or pivotal moments in the story. Ask students to identify the main message in the book and how the message translates in this new format.

Teacher Prompts
- Do we interpret media messages differently when we listen than we do when we read?
- Is the message the same in both media forms?
- Did you pick up new details in the text or messages by creating the audio version?
- What parts worked better as a book?
- What parts worked better as an audio book?
- How does bringing dialogue to life change the book?

Photo Book

Reinforce with students that media messages can be communicated without words. Have students create a story of their choice using photographs or illustrations. It could be about anything such as a soccer game, an art show, or a trip to the mall. The elements of a story: sequence (beginning, middle, and ending), setting (when and where the story takes place), and characters (thing, people, or places).

A Picture Is...

Ask students to paint a picture or snap a photograph of something in their neighbourhood. Ask them to give it a catchy headline, along with a cutline to describe what is happening in the picture. Visual elements such as photographs and illustrations are key elements used in newspapers and magazines. Have students look through periodicals for inspiration.

Write a Text Message Using Emoticons

Talking on cell phones is nothing new. These days, everyone is texting. So what is texting, and how do people communicate through text messages? Below are some popular emoticons—symbols that represent emotions—commonly used in text messages and emails.

:) happy	:(sad	=O shocked	>:-(mad
=D laughing out loud	:@ screaming	:-\ undecided	B-) cool
;) winking or kidding	:'(crying	:-] grinning	:x not talking

As a class, use emoticons to write a text message about an upcoming school trip or activity.

Build a Class Website

Investing the time to create a class website is definitely worthwhile. Use the website as a springboard for all the wonderful things happening in your classroom.

Design a CD Cover

Have students design a CD cover for their fictional band. Students will have to be creative and think of a band name, what type of music they play, a colour scheme for the cover, and the name of the album. Students should be reminded that, if their music will be featured online, the same cover will be used to sell digital copies. So they need to think about how to attract their target audience. If possible, provide empty CD cases for students to use. Students can use **BLM 31: Using Colour to Help Sell a Product** to help them design their CD cover.

Write a Jingle

As a class, listen to a few radio commercials and create a broadcast jingle for a toy. Jingles are catchy; they usually rhyme, and are very short. Students can use instruments in the class for sound effects. They can also record the jingle and play it back to hear the finished product.

Print Advertisement

Have students design a print advertisement. Be sure to encourage them to consider design, font, colour elements, and content when assembling the print advertisement. Some ideas for a print advertisement are to announce an event, promote a service, advocate a point of view, or sell a product. As a class, brainstorm a list of persuasive words students can use in their advertisement. Students can also use **BLM 32: Tips for Print Advertisements** to start their thinking. The teacher may wish to have students try to communicate the same message for different target audiences, or using different persuasive techniques. This will make a great springboard for discussion.

Oral Presentation

Have students use **BLM 33: Oral Presentation Outline** to prepare for a public speaking activity, or as a response to something they have viewed or read.

Video Presentation

Have students create a video presentation such as a newscast, commercial, or public service announcement.

Restaurant Menu

Have students examine several examples of menus from a variety of restaurants. Brainstorm a list of characteristics that can be seen in most menus. Discuss the persuasive language and visual elements that make menus appealing. Then have students create their own restaurant menus with a target audience in mind.

Greeting Card

Brainstorm with students a list of reasons why people give greeting cards. Then have students decide on a message for their card and create it.

Blog Entry

Review with the class the features of a blog. Then encourage students to write their own blog entry about an event in their life. Blogs can look very much like letters with a greeting, personal anecdotes, and photographs. The tone is informal and conversational.

Review a Book, Play, or Movie

Using the teacher prompts below as a guideline, have students write their own review of a book, play, or movie. Students can use **BLM 34: Write a Review** to guide their writing.

- What was it about?
- What was the genre—drama, comedy, suspense?
- When and where did it take place?
- How convincing were the characters or actors?
- How did the plot unfold?
- What did you like about it? State your reasons.
- What did you dislike about it? State your reasons.
- What elements, such as sound effects, voice over, descriptive language, lighting, or music helped to deliver the message?

Opinion Piece

Letters to the editors can be found in newspapers and magazines. These letters can be in response to an article, or about an issue that has personal significance. Ask students to write a persuasive letter about an issue or subject that matters to them. Have students research the issue using at least three different types of media such as magazines, books, and the Internet. As a class, brainstorm a list of persuasive words students can use to convince readers of their point of view. Discuss as a class what types of publications they could submit the letter to. Note: This can be an individual or class exercise.

Teacher Prompts
- What are the main features of writing a persuasive letter?
- What is the difference between fact and opinion?
- Why is this issue important to you?
- How else can we spread a message about an issue?
- Who is the intended audience for this letter?
- What is the tone of the letter?
- Have you ever written a letter for a cause?

Write a Magazine Article

Ask students to write a magazine article about something that interests them. Have students research to find information to make their article interesting. They can use **BLM 35: Magazine Article Checklist** to make sure they have covered all the elements of a good magazine article.

Signs and Symbols

Review with students how it is possible to communicate a message without using words. Brainstorm a list of examples such as signs or symbols in your community. Then challenge students to create their own signs or symbols to communicate a specific message

Dear _____:

Some newspapers and magazines contain advice columns where people can write in to ask for advice about a problem or situation they are facing. Brainstorm with students some situations for which people might ask for advice. Have students choose from the list or think of another topic, and use **BLM 36: A Letter of Advice** to write their letter. You may wish to invite students to share their letters with the class.

Create a Brochure

Have students create a brochure to serve a specific purpose. It can provide information, advertise a product or service, share a belief or viewpoint, or draw attention to a cause. Students can use **BLM 37: Brilliant Brochure** for steps and a checklist for creating their brochure. You may wish to invite students to share their finished brochure with the class.

Make a Statement!

T-shirts are often created to state a group or organization's collective feelings—positive or negative. They are sold to raise funds, and worn to draw attention to a specific cause or issue. These causes or issues are often things people disagree with or do not like—things they are trying to change. Students can create their own T-shirt to share their views about something they would like to change in the world. They can use **BLM 38: _____ T-shirt** to create a statement T-shirt of their own. Invite students to share their creations with the class.

Welcome Home

Encourage students' creativity by giving them the opportunity to design and draw their dream home. After designing their home, students will assume the role of a real estate agent to sell the home they created. Students can use any media text they prefer to create an appealing advertisement for potential homebuyers. They can use **BLM 39: Design and Sell Your Dream Home** to draw their home and guide their work. They can also use **BLM 28: Media Text Planner** to help them create their advertisement.

Create a Magazine

Have students work in small groups to design and create a 10-page magazine. Students should decide who their target audience will be, then choose a theme for their magazine. They can brainstorm ideas for articles, photographs or drawings, advertisements, and other features that would appeal to their target audience. Students can design and create an attention-grabbing cover, with teaser headlines to interest readers. **BLM 40: Create a Magazine** can be used as a checklist to help groups create a top-quality magazine.

Design a Poster

Posters advertise many things, such as concerts, CDs, movies, television shows, clothing, perfume, beauty products, foods, drinks, stores, vehicles, and vacation destinations. They also advertise upcoming events. Have students create a poster to advertise something from the above list, or of their own choosing. Remind them to use persuasive words and phrases. Students can use **BLM 41: Poster Checklist** to help them create an interesting, persuasive, and eye-catching poster.

Create a Board Game

Have students work in groups to develop an idea for a new board game. They can use **BLM 42: Create a Board Game** to give them ideas and steps to follow to create their game. Students can invite another group to play their finished game. Reinforce with students that they should consider the purpose and target audience for their game. You may also wish to challenge students to create a commercial or print advertisement for their game.

Media Text Planner

Type of Media Text _____

What is the main purpose? _____ **Inform** _____ **Persuade** _____ **Entertain**	Details:
Who is the target audience?	Details:
What is in my message?	Details:
What do I need to include in this media text?	Details:
What persuasive techniques will I use to grab the attention of my audience?	Details:

Tips for Creating Media Texts

What is my purpose for creating this media text?

Is your purpose to inform, entertain, or persuade? Are you creating a media text to achieve more than one of these purposes? If so, consider whether one of the purposes is more important to you.

Who is my target audience?

Is there a particular group that you want to read, view, or listen to your media text? Consider age, gender (male or female), and interests. Your target audience might be a large group, such as any adult. Or your target audience might be more specific, such as girls between the ages of 10 and 14 who like skateboarding.

How should I communicate my message?

1. *How much content do I need to include to achieve my purpose(s)?*
   For example, if your message is short and simple, a poster might work. If you have lots of information to communicate, perhaps a booklet would work better.

2. *What form will allow me to reach my target audience?*
   If you want to sell a product to children, a television commercial would work better than a print ad in a magazine. Most children watch television, but many children do not read magazines.

continued next page ☞

3. *What form will work best with my content?*

If your content will include labelled diagrams, you will want these to be large enough for people to easily read them. If you create a computer slide presentation and put each diagram on a different slide, the diagrams will be large and easy to read. If you try to fit diagrams and some text on a one-page handout, your diagrams will have to be much smaller.

How can I make my media text visually interesting?

People are more likely to pay attention if the media text is visually interesting. If you film a video of yourself giving a presentation, wear a bright colour rather than an outfit that is all black. Do not stand still like a statue—change your facial expression and use body language to help keep your audience interested. If you are creating a print text or a webpage, think about including visuals such as photographs. Consider different ways to use colour, and decide whether you should use a couple of different fonts rather than just one.

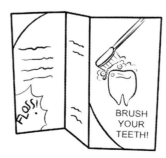

Media Text Self-Evaluation

Use this page to reflect on a media text you have created.

My media text: _____

Purpose: _____

Form: _____ **Target audience:** _____

1. In what ways was your media text most successful?

_____

_____

_____

2. In what ways could your media text be more successful?

_____

_____

_____

3. What was the biggest challenge in creating this media text?

_____

_____

_____

4. What was the most important thing you learned from creating this media text?

_____

_____

_____

Using Colour to Help Sell a Product

Colours and Their Meanings

RED — Energy, excitement, momentum, strength, power, warmth, love, anger, danger, fire, aggression, passion.

YELLOW — Joy, happiness, hopefulness, optimism, imagination, sunshine, summer, gold, dishonesty, fear, betrayal, envy, illness.

BLUE — Harmony, peace, calm, steadiness, unity, trust, confidence, cleanliness, order, security, loyalty, sky, water, cold, technology, sadness.

ORANGE — Energy, balance, warmth, enthusiasm, expansive, glitzy, attention-grabbing.

GREEN — Nature, environment, healthy, good luck, renewal, youth, vitality, spring, generosity, fertility, jealousy, inexperience, hardship.

PURPLE — Royalty, spirituality, nobility, mysterious, transformation, wisdom, enlightenment, cruelty, arrogance, mourning.

GREY — Safety, dependability, intelligence, modesty, maturity, old-fashioned, practical, depression, boredom.

WHITE — Admiration, purity, minimalism, cleanliness, peace, innocence, youth, birth, winter, snow, virtue, hygiene.

BROWN — Earth, home, outdoors, trustworthiness, comfort, staying power, strength, simplicity, calm.

BLACK — Power, dominance, formality, elegance, wealth, mystery, terror, evil, anonymity, unhappiness, sadness, remorse, death.

continued next page ☞

Create an advertisement for one of the following:

- vacation
- cereal
- car
- clothing
- perfume
- home
- safety message
- public service announcement
- restaurant

Think about what colour scheme might engage the target audience and persuade them to buy your product.

What you need

- paper
- colouring material
- "Using Colour to Help Sell a Product" page

What is your advertisement going to be about?

_____

_____

_____

_____

What colours are you going to use and why?

_____

_____

_____

_____

_____

Tips for Print Advertisements

1. Include a memorable headline:

Create a catchy phrase that will help people remember your message. For example, "Ocean Cruises—this is the life!"

2. Graphics should be eye-catching:

Choose graphics that will help communicate your message. For example, a picture of the ocean will create an impression of peacefulness. The colours you choose are important too!

3. Carefully plan the text:

The type and size of font you choose will help communicate your message. Plan the location of the words on the paper carefully so that people will read it.

4. Include an attractive logo:

Craft a visual sign or symbol to represent the manufacturer or group. For example, a ship with a wave under it could be used to represent a cruise line.

5. Use the whole space to your advantage:

Make sure every part of the ad space helps people focus on your message. Blank areas are fine.

Ocean Cruises—this is the life!

All of the top celebrities choose our cruises!

Book Now! Get 40% Off!

OC

Oral Presentation Outline

Topic: _____

Target audience: _____

Purpose: _____

How long does it need to be? _____

Introduction Checklist

I introduced my topic in an attention-grabbing way, such as

❑ a quote

❑ a statistic

❑ an example

❑ a question

❑ I state what I am going to talk about in 1 to 3 sentences.

continued next page ☞

Body Checklist

❑ My main point has supporting details, examples, or descriptions.

❑ I wrote out my ideas the way I would sound if I were explaining, showing, or telling someone in person during a conversation.

❑ I read aloud what I wrote.

Tip: You do not have to use full sentences. Write it the same way you talk.

Main point:

Supporting details:

continued next page ☞

Conclusion Checklist

❑ I summarized my key points.

❑ I ended my oral presentation in an attention-grabbing way, such as

    ❑ a quote

    ❑ a statistic

    ❑ a question

_____

_____

_____

_____

_____

_____

_____

_____

Presentation Delivery Tips

• Practise! Practise! Practise! Get comfortable with what you have written.

• Highlight your good copy in places where you would like to pause for effect, or emphasize a point.

• Think about hand gestures and making eye contact with the audience or camera.

• Think about your tone of voice to show enthusiasm, emotion, or volume.

Write a Review

Share your opinion about a book, play, or movie.

Title of Media: _____

Type of Media: _____

Outline the Main Idea:

_____

_____

_____

In My Opinion:

_____

_____

_____

_____

_____

_____

_____

_____

_____

_____

☐ Recommended

☐ Not recommended

Reviewed by:

_____

Magazine Article Checklist

Parts of an Article

- The **HEADLINE** names the article.
- The **BYLINE** shows the name of the author. (You)
- The **BEGINNING** gives the most important idea.
- The **MIDDLE** gives supporting details about the idea.
- The **ENDING** usually gives the reader an idea to remember.

Article Checklist

CONTENT

- ☐ I have a **HEADLINE** that names the article.
- ☐ I have a **BYLINE** that shows my name as the author.
- ☐ I have a **BEGINNING** that gives the most important ideas.
- ☐ I have a **MIDDLE** that give supporting details about the idea.
- ☐ I have an **ENDING** that gives the reader an idea to remember.

GRAMMAR AND STYLE

- ☐ I used my neatest printing and included a clear title.
- ☐ I included a colourful drawing or photograph to support my article.
- ☐ I spelled my words correctly.
- ☐ I used interesting words.
- ☐ I checked that I used capitals, periods, commas, and question marks correctly.

A Letter of Advice

People ask for advice when they have a problem or would like an opinion about something. Give some advice to someone about a specific situation. Explain your thinking to convince the person that your advice is the right thing to do.

I am giving advice to _____

about _____

Dear _____,

_____

_____

_____

_____

_____

_____

_____

_____

_____

_____

_____

_____

Your friend,

_____

Brilliant Brochure

A *brochure* is a booklet or pamphlet that contains descriptive information. Choose a topic for your brochure. Topics may include something that you are studying in school or something that interests you.

STEP 1: Plan Your Brochure

STEP	COMPLETION
1. Take a piece of paper and fold the paper the same way your brochure will be folded.	
2. • Before writing the brochure, plan the layout in pencil. • Write the heading for each section where you would like it to be in the brochure. • Leave room underneath each section to write information. • Also leave room for graphics or drawings.	

STEP 2: Complete a Draft

STEP	COMPLETION
1. Research information for each section of your brochure.	
2. Read your draft for meaning, then add, delete, or change words to improve your writing.	

STEP 3: Final Editing Checklist

☐ I checked the spelling. ☐ My brochure is neat and organized.

☐ I checked the punctuation. ☐ My brochure has drawings or graphics.

☐ I checked for clear sentences. ☐ My brochure is attractive.

T-shirt

_____

Design a T-shirt that communicates a message.

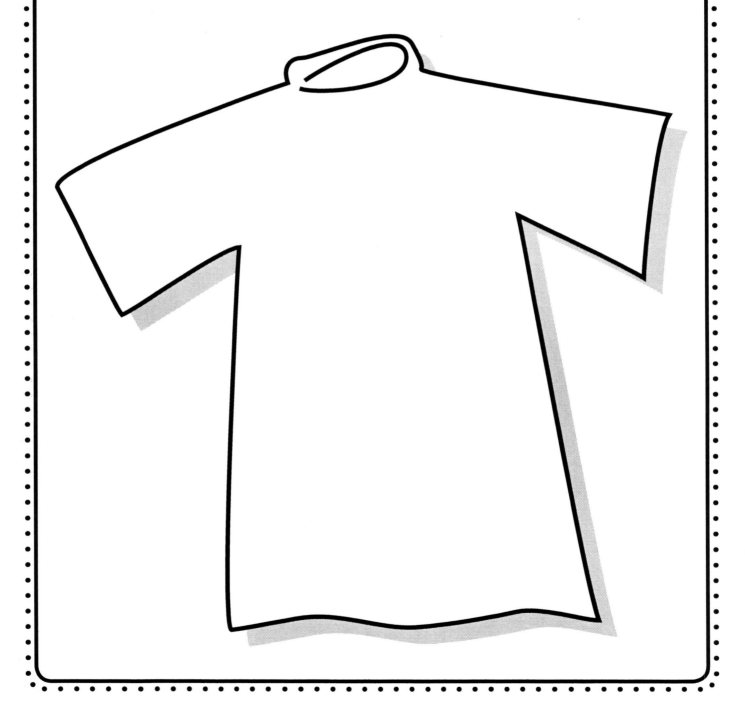

Design and Sell Your Dream Home

Design and draw your dream home. Make sure you include details.

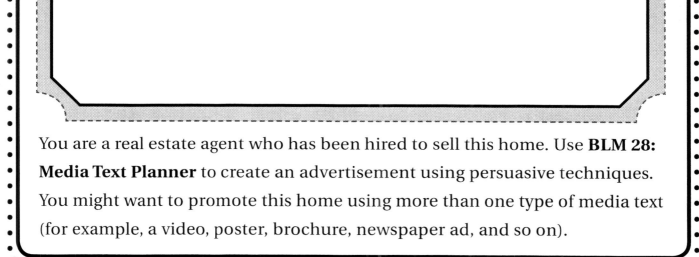

You are a real estate agent who has been hired to sell this home. Use **BLM 28: Media Text Planner** to create an advertisement using persuasive techniques. You might want to promote this home using more than one type of media text (for example, a video, poster, brochure, newspaper ad, and so on).

Create a Magazine

Here is a checklist for a top-quality magazine.

Magazine Cover

☐ The title of the magazine is easy to read and prominent on the cover.

☐ There is an attractive illustration to let readers know the theme of the magazine.

☐ There are 1 or 2 magazine highlight statements about what is inside the magazine.

Editor's Page

☐ The letter is addressed to the readers.

☐ The letter lets readers know why you think it is important for them to read your magazine.

Table of Contents

☐ There is a complete listing of what is in the magazine.

Advertisements

☐ There are student-created advertisements throughout the magazine.

Magazine Articles

☐ _____

☐ _____

☐ _____

☐ _____

☐ _____

☐ Point of View

Visual Appeal

☐ The magazine has neat and colourful drawings, and other labelled diagrams.

Other article ideas and columns to include in your magazine:

• advice column   • an interview   • biography of a famous citizen   • survey and results

continued next page ☞

Group members: _____

Use this magazine plan to assign jobs to each group member.

Job	Group Member	Complete

Poster Checklist

Topic: _____

Purpose of Poster: _____

Poster Appeal	❑ The layout design is eye-catching. ❑ The heading grabs the reader's attention.
Purpose and Content	❑ The message is clear. ❑ There are supporting facts, details, and/or descriptions.
Target Audience	❑ The target audience for the poster is clear.
Visuals	❑ The visuals support the purpose of the poster. ❑ The visuals are appealing.
Assigned Poster Requirements	❑ I completed all parts of the assignment.
Proofreading	❑ I checked the spelling. ❑ I checked the punctuation. ❑ I used different types of sentence.

Additional Notes:

_____

_____

_____

Create a Board Game

Create your own board game! Base your game on a theme that you are studying in class or something that interests you.

WHAT YOU NEED

- a base for the game board, such as a large piece of construction paper, a clean takeout pizza box, or file folder
- colouring materials

- scissors
- glue
- construction paper
- 2 number cubes

WHAT YOU DO

1. Choose a theme for your game.
2. Create a path the game pieces will follow. You may choose to give your path a specific shape: a U-shape, an L-shape, a square, or an oval. Make your path at least 50 squares long.
3. Add spaces where you have to stack question cards cut from heavy paper. Print or handwrite questions on the cards.
4. Test the game to see if it is too hard or has enough spaces.
5. Cut small figures out of paper to use as game pieces, or use materials that are available.
6. Decorate your game board to make it colourful and eye-catching.
7. Write rules and directions on how to play your game.

Rules and How to Play

- How does a player move around the board? Here are some ideas:
  - roll the number cubes
  - pick up a card and answer a question
  - follow the instructions on the game board spaces
- How many people can play?
- Are there penalties for wrong answers?

Ideas for Game Cards

- math questions
- true or false
- answer the question
- multiple choice

A Web Organizer About...

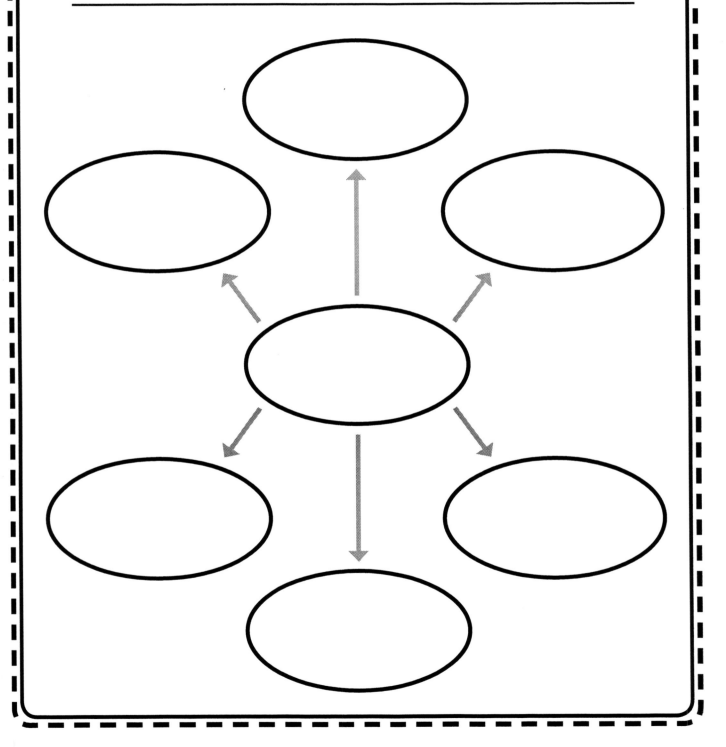

Writing Planner

Topic—Introduction

Idea—Paragraph 1

Idea—Paragraph 2

Supporting Detail

Supporting Detail

Supporting Detail

Supporting Detail

Concluding Paragraph

Media Expert!

_____

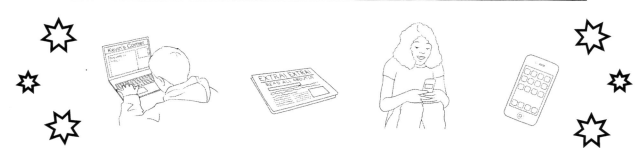

You are unbelievable!

Great Work!

_____

Keep up the effort!

Rubric 1: Oral Presentation

	Level 1 Below Expectations	Level 2 Approaching Expectations	Level 3 Meets Expectations	Level 4 Exceeds Expectations
Presentation Style	• Infrequently uses gestures, eye contact, and tone of voice to engage the audience. • Does not hold the attention of the audience. • Is not prepared.	• Sometimes uses gestures, eye contact, and tone of voice to engage the audience. • Holds the attention of the audience for some of the presentation. • Is somewhat prepared and lacks confidence.	• Usually uses gestures, eye contact, and tone of voice to engage the audience. • Holds the attention of the audience for most of the presentation. • Is well prepared and confident.	• Successfully uses gestures, eye contact, and tone of voice to engage the audience. • Holds the attention of the audience for all of the presentation. • Is thoroughly prepared and confident.
Purpose	• Purpose of the presentation is not established. • The message is unclear.	• Purpose of the presentation is somewhat apparent. • The message is somewhat clear.	• Purpose of the presentation is apparent. • The message is clear.	• Purpose of the presentation is clear. • The message is obviously clear.
Content	• Exhibits little content knowledge. • Content lacks organization and contains abrupt transitions.	• Exhibits limited content knowledge. • Content is somewhat organized with few evident transitions.	• Shows content knowledge. • Content is organized with evident transitions.	• Shows thorough content knowledge. • Content is organized with fluid transitions.
Assignment Requirements	• Assignment requirements are incomplete.	• More than half of the assignment requirements are fulfilled.	• Assignment requirements are fulfilled.	• Assignment requirements are fulfilled in extended ways.

Rubric 2: Brilliant Brochure

	Level 1 Below Expectations	Level 2 Approaching Expectations	Level 3 Meets Expectations	Level 4 Exceeds Expectations
Content	• Less than half of the sections in the brochure are complete. • Little of the content is accurate.	• More than half of the sections in the brochure are complete. • The content is accurate to a certain extent.	• Almost all of the sections in the brochure are complete. • All of the content is accurate.	• Each section of the brochure is complete. • All of the content is accurate with added detail.
Brochure Appeal	• Brochure layout is not organized and is confusing for the reader.	• Brochure layout is fairly organized.	• Brochure layout is organized and eye-catching.	• Brochure layout is very organized and very eye-catching.
Purpose	• Purpose of the brochure is not established. • The message is unclear.	• Purpose of the brochure is somewhat apparent. • The message is somewhat clear.	• Purpose of the brochure is apparent. • The message is clear.	• Purpose of the brochure is obvious. • The message is obviously clear.
Visual Elements	• Very few graphics support the information.	• Some graphics support the information.	• Most graphics support the information.	• Graphics successfully support the information.
Proofreading	• There are several spelling or grammar errors.	• There are some spelling or grammar errors.	• There are few spelling or grammar errors.	• There are no spelling or grammar errors.

Rubric 3: Print Advertisement

	Level 1 Below Expectations	Level 2 Approaching Expectations	Level 3 Meets Expectations	Level 4 Exceeds Expectations
Poster Appeal	• Poor design. Layout is unattractive and messy.	• Basic design. Layout and neatness are acceptable.	• Interesting design. Layout and neatness are good.	• Very well-thought-out design. Excellent layout and neatness.
Content	• Few facts are accurately displayed on the poster.	• Some facts are accurately displayed on the poster.	• Most facts are accurately displayed on the poster.	• Facts are accurately displayed on the poster.
Graphic Support	• No graphics are related to the topic and no support of the information.	• Few graphics are related to the topic and little support of the information.	• Most graphics are related to the topic and support the information.	• Graphics are related to the topic and support the information.
Assigned Poster Requirements	• Several elements were missing. No additional information was added.	• Some of the necessary elements are included, but no additional information.	• Most of the necessary elements are included, as well as some additional information.	• All necessary elements are included, as well as additional information.

Rubric 4: Create a Magazine

	Level 1 Below Expectations	Level 2 Approaching Expectations	Level 3 Meets Expectations	Level 4 Exceeds Expectations
Content	• Limited information. • Few supporting details.	• Some of the required information. • Some supporting details.	• Most of the required information. • Accurate and complete supporting details.	• Comprehensive information. • Very thorough supporting details.
Writing Conventions	• Many spelling and grammar errors, and inconsistent punctuation in the good copy.	• Some of the spelling, grammar, and punctuation are correct in the good copy.	• Most of the spelling, grammar, and punctuation are correct in the good copy.	• All of the spelling, grammar, and punctuation are correct in the good copy.
Graphics/Pictures	• Pictures rarely match the information. • No use of colour enhancement.	• Some pictures match the information. • Some use of colour enhancement.	• Pictures are complete and appropriate. • Considerable use of colour enhancement.	• Pictures are outstanding and consistently match the information. • Eye-catching and purposeful use of colour enhancement.
Overall Presentation	• Little organization or neatness.	• Some organization and neatness.	• General organization and neatness.	• Outstanding organization and neatness.

Rubric 5: Media Concepts

	Level 1 Below Expectations	Level 2 Approaching Expectations	Level 3 Meets Expectations	Level 4 Exceeds Expectations
Student Participation	• Rarely contributes to class discussions and activities by offering ideas and asking questions.	• Sometimes contributes to class discussions and activities by offering ideas and asking questions.	• Usually contributes to class discussions and activities by offering ideas and asking questions.	• Consistently contributes to class discussions and activities by offering ideas and asking questions.
Understanding of Concepts	• Shows little understanding of concepts and rarely gives complete explanations. • Intensive teacher support is needed.	• Shows a satisfactory understanding of most concepts and sometimes gives appropriate, but incomplete explanations. • Teacher support is sometimes needed	• Shows a good understanding of most concepts and usually gives complete or nearly complete explanations. • Infrequent teacher support is needed.	• Shows a thorough understanding of all or almost all concepts and consistently gives appropriate and complete explanations independently. • No teacher support is needed.
Communication of Concepts	• Rarely communicates with clarity and precision in written and oral work, or uses appropriate terminology and vocabulary.	• Sometimes communicates with clarity and precision in written and oral work, and uses appropriate terminology and vocabulary.	• Usually communicates with clarity and precision in written and oral work, and uses appropriate terminology and vocabulary.	• Consistently communicates with clarity and precision in written and oral work, and uses appropriate terminology and vocabulary.

Media Literacy Glossary

Advertising   Calling attention to a product, service, need, etc. It is often a paid announcement on websites or billboards, over radio or television, or in newspapers or magazines.

Audience   Intended consumers, listeners, readers, or viewers for a particular media text.

Bias   Tendency or inclination. Bias may prevent a person from looking at an issue with an open mind.

Blogs   Personal journals published on the Internet. Blog is short for *weblog*.

Brand loyalty   A person's preference for a product. Companies work hard to make customers loyal to their products.

Browsers   Software programs that let you find, see, and hear material on the Internet. Examples of browsers include Internet Explorer, Firefox, Safari, etc. Also called Web browsers.

CD-ROMs (Compact Disc Read-Only Memory)   Computer discs that can store large amounts of information but cannot record or save it.

Chat rooms   Branches of a computer network that allow participants to communicate in real-time discussions.

Connotations   Descriptions of ideology, meaning, or value that are associated with media text.

Consumers   People who buy goods or services and use them personally, rather than selling them.

Conventions   Accepted practises or rules in the use of language. Conventions can include capital letters, punctuation, headings, etc. See also *text features*.

Critical thinking   Ability to question and understand issues presented in advertisements, print, television, etc.

Cyberspace   Electronic communication on the Internet and other computer networks, and the culture developing around them.

Deconstruct   To break down a media text into its parts to understand how and why it was created.

Demographics   Characteristics or data about a group of people, including age, gender, education, income, etc.

Digital media   Electronic devices and media platforms on which people can create and store media texts, and interact with others. Digital media includes cell phones, computers, Internet, social networking websites, etc.

Discussion groups   Online areas that are focused on specific topics. Users can read other people's comments and add their own comments.

Elements of text   Characteristics of a specific text form, including characters, setting, story, and more.

Emails   Messages sent electronically between computer users. *Email* stands for "electronic mail."

Emoticons   Symbols people use in emails and chat rooms to show an emotion. For example, :) means "I am happy."

Facts   Things that actually exist.

FAQs (Frequently Asked Questions)   Questions and answers about a specific topic, such as mailing lists, products, websites, etc.

Flaming   Insulting people or criticizing them angrily in an electronic message.

Focus groups   Small groups of people chosen by marketers to test new advertisements, products, or services. Marketers use these groups to try to learn how a larger group will react.

Genre   Media texts that have a specific content, form, or style.

Hardware   Electrical, electronic, magnetic, and mechanical devices in a computer system, including the disk drives, keyboard, and screen.

Home pages   Initial pages of websites on the Internet.

HTML (Hypertext Markup Language)   Formatting or standards used in documents on the Internet.

Hyperlinks Links or cross-references from one electronic document to another electronic document or to a webpage.

Hypertext Method of storing data through a computer program that lets users make and link information.

Ideology Beliefs that guide a group or institution.

IM (Instant Messaging) System for exchanging typed electronic messages instantly via a cellular network or the Internet.

Industry Groups involved in the production of media texts.

Internet World's largest system of linked computers.

ISP (Internet Service Provider) Company that can connect you directly to the Internet.

Jolts Moments in a media text generated by comedy, loud noises, rapid editing, and more. These jolts are included to interest and excite the audience.

Marketing The many ways products are sold. Marketing includes advertising, selling, and delivering products to people.

Mass media Communication aimed at a very large audience. Mass media includes the Internet, magazines, television, and more.

Media Forms of communication, including CD-ROMs, magazines, television, and websites. (*Media* is the plural of *medium*.)

Media conventions and techniques Creating specific effects using images and sounds to convey the message in a text. Examples of effects include using animation, colour, logos, special effects, and more.

Media education Learning how to create media texts, as well as how to interpret them.

Media forms Formats used to communicate a message. Media forms can include blogs, movies, product packaging, and more.

Media literacy Understanding of media and the techniques used by them.

Media texts Images, sound, text, or visuals (or combinations of these) that are used to communicate a message.

Medium Form of communication, such as the Internet, radio, or television. (The plural of *medium* is *media*.)

Multimedia Combination of two or more forms of media, such as audio, images, text, and video.

Narratives Telling of a plot or story. In a media text, narrative is the coherent sequence of events.

Net All of cyberspace, including commercial services, the Internet, etc.

Netiquette Rules of behaviour or etiquette that apply when using computer networks, especially the Internet.

Newbies New users of a technology.

Online communication Communicating over the Internet or through a commercial network.

Opinions Attitudes or beliefs, often not based on facts.

Point of view Attitude or opinion. Point of view affects how events are acted on or seen.

Posting Sending an electronic message to a discussion group or other message area.

Print and electronic resources Information or reference materials that are in print or electronic media. These resources include books, databases, videos, and more.

Print media Any media text produced on paper. Can also include such usages as a blimp with a company logo, and may contain only photographs without words.

Product placement Advertising that involves marketers paying to have their product shown in the media.

Production Process of creating media texts. Also, the people who create media texts.

Representation Process of media texts describing and standing for ideas, people, places, or real events.

Search engines   Programs on some websites that can search for information on the Internet, based on supplied words or phrases.

Servers   Computers that provide data or software programs to other machines linked to it in a network.

Social networks   Online communities of people who use a website or other technologies to communicate.

Software   Programs used to direct the operation of computers. Systems software, such as Mac OS and Windows, operate computers. Application software has such uses as playing games, word processing, etc.

Spam   Unwanted email on the Internet.

Stereotypes   Simplified, standardized images of people or things.

Storyboards   Sequences of sketches used to plan an advertisement, movie, television show, or video.

Target audience   Specific group of people expected to buy a particular product or service.

Technology   Machinery, materials, and tools used to create a media text. Technology can have a big impact on the connotation and construction of a media text.

Text   Communication that uses words, sounds, or images to present information. Can be in electronic, oral, print, or visual form. Also, to send a text message.

Text features   Characteristics of a text that clarify the text, including fonts, headings, and illustrations. See also *conventions*.

Text messages   Usually very short messages sent electronically. Text messages often contain short forms and emoticons.

URL (Uniform Resource Locator)   Address of a website on the Internet.

Values   Personal views or judgments about what is important in life.

Webcasts   Broadcasts or recordings of events on the Internet.

Webpages   Pages of information at a website. Webpages can include graphics, hyperlinks, text, and more.

WebQuests   Inquiries in which most or all of the information gathered is drawn from the Internet.

Websites   Collections of webpages. These pages may include graphics, sounds, and links to other websites. A website may cover one topic or many topics.

Answers to BLM Questions

BLM 1: What Is Media? (pp. 8–9)

1. **a)** Restroom sign: Both women and men can use this washroom. **b)** Poison symbol: This could make you very sick or kill you if you drink or eat it. **c)** Traffic signal: Stop at a red light, slow down for a yellow light, or go when the light is green. **d)** Litter symbol: Do not drop your trash on the ground. **e)** Walk sign: It is now safe to walk across the street. **f)** Wheelchair symbol: This indicates special parking spaces or areas that are made accessible for people who use a wheelchair.

2. Sample answers: Media is used in daily life to keep up with the news on the radio, on the Internet, or in the newspaper; create a list, leave a note for someone, make a note to remind yourself to do something, make a warning sign, write a diary or journal entry, phone someone, send a text message, write an email.

3. **a)** The purposes are to inform (provide people with reasons to eat different vegetables), to entertain (by making the lyrics funny), and to persuade (as suggested by the song's title and the inclusion of reasons to eat different vegetables). **b)** the Internet **c)** music video; Sample answers: A music video upload was a good choice. Many people will probably see it, and they can hear the song instead of just reading the lyrics. Jeff can also use facial expressions and gestures to make the song even funnier and to get his message across.

4. Answers will vary.

Media Word Search (p. 12)

E	L	I	T	E	L	E	V	I	S	I	O	N	P
O	P	C	O	M	I	C	M	S	B	P	H	O	R
D	O	P	L	S	E	N	R	O	A	G	S	F	N
V	D	B	A	C	B	I	T	I	V	T	U	L	E
I	C	I	L	L	G	R	W	E	E	I	P	Y	W
D	A	L	S	O	L	A	O	R	R	O	E	E	S
E	S	L	P	L	G	D	M	C	B	N	E	R	P
O	T	B	E	L	D	I	E	S	H	D	E	C	A
G	C	O	E	B	O	O	N	B	A	U	E	T	P
A	O	A	C	W	H	G	U	E	C	R	R	A	E
M	E	R	H	G	R	B	O	O	K	W	T	E	R
E	A	D	V	E	R	T	I	S	E	M	E	N	T
P	O	P	H	O	T	O	G	R	A	P	H	B	L

BLM 6: Why Is It Important to Learn About Media? (pp. 19–20)

1. **a)** Being popular is the most important thing. **b)** The ad wants young people to buy the jeans. **c)** The ad wants to make young people believe that buying the jeans will make them the most popular person in the class. **d)** Answers may vary; Sample answers: Is being popular really the most important thing to me? Can wearing a certain type of jeans really make someone more popular?

2. **a)** Answers will vary. If necessary, prompt students to list specific elements and techniques, such as use of humour, background music or sound effects, a catchy jingle, lots of fast-paced action, or the appearance of a celebrity or popular cartoon character.

BLM 8: Media Purposes (p. 28)

1. **a)** inform (by listing the vitamins), persuade (most commercials persuade people to buy things), entertain (by including funny cartoon characters), make money (by getting people to buy the cereal)
   b) entertain (with music and lyrics), make money (for the record company and the artist)
   c) inform (about a student's progress in school; Some students might reasonably suggest that comments on a report card might try to persuade a student to keep up the good work or try harder.)
   d) inform (tell people what products are on sale, at what prices), persuade (convince people to shop at the store), make money (for the store owner)
   e) inform (to teach students about math), make money (for the company that published the book)
   f) inform (warn people it is dangerous to proceed)
   g) inform (give the time the party will start and directions to get there)
   h) inform (let people know about the new type of running shoes), persuade (by making the wearer look interesting), entertain (by showing amazing skateboard tricks), make money (for the shoe company)

i) inform (tells about the puppy and shows a photograph, states the reward, and gives a number to call if you find the puppy), persuade (the reward might persuade someone who found the puppy to return it, or might persuade people to look for the puppy)

j) inform (lets people know that they should not park there), persuade (letting people know that their car will be towed might persuade people not to park there)

BLM 9: Media Forms (p. 31)

1. a) Answers will vary. Sample answers: a blog or website (with photographs and/or embedded videos), a photograph album (with captions), an oral presentation (with photograph slides and/or video clips), a personal essay (with photographs), a book (with photographs), a video (compilation of video clips with narration)

   b) Answers will vary. Students might suggest that a form that can include text (spoken or written), photographs, and videos would do the best job of communicating information about the trip.

2. Sample answers: opening theme music, a host, contestants, questions to answer or tasks that must be performed, prizes (including cash), time for the host to introduce the contestants or for the contestants to introduce themselves, multiple rounds of questions or tasks, commercial breaks

3. Sample answers: a photograph or illustration for each month, the name of the month is presented in large letters at the top of each page, the calendar for each month is presented as a grid or chart, the day of the week is listed at the top of each column, weeks always begin on a Sunday, holidays are noted on the appropriate dates, each day is presented in a square that leaves space for people to make notes

BLM 10: The Target Audience (p. 34)

1. a–c) Answers will vary, depending on the commercial chosen.

2. a) students in the class, parents of students in the class, possibly students in other classes in the school

   b) the judges of the contest, audience members

   c) friends and relatives invited to the party

d) students, school staff, parents of students, people in the community

e) people who have a garden and are interested in growing vegetables

f) parents of young children

BLM 12: Print Media (p. 41)

1. Sample answers: poster, map, catalogue, paper money, postage stamp, report card, event or travel ticket

2. Answers will vary.

3. This type of billboard is not an example of print media because it is not printed on paper.

4. Answers will vary.

BLM 14: Digital Media (p. 49)

1. Answers will vary.

2. Answers will vary.

BLM 24: Persuasive Techniques (pp. 73–74)

1. a) present an expert's opinion

   b) make people afraid

   c) present a testimonial

   d) present only some of the facts

   e) exaggerate

   f) present a testimonial

2. Answers will vary. Sample answers:

   a) Cereal for kids: jump on the bandwagon ("Everyone loves this cereal!"), exaggerate ("This is the BEST cereal ever!")

   b) Gym membership for adults: present a testimonial (show other people who have gotten in shape at the gym, or who have improved their health), jump on the bandwagon ("Everyone is working out these days."), exaggerate (claim people shaped up in a very short time)

   c) Jeans for teenagers: jump on the bandwagon ("All the cool kids wear these jeans."), present a testimonial (a teenager says, "I love these jeans!"), exaggerate ("These are the most comfortable jeans ever made."), make people afraid (show teenagers wearing the new jeans whispering about someone who is not wearing them)